More Praise for *Winning Under Fire*

"When you read about Dale Collie's fantastic background, you will see why he has earned the right to teach us about leadership. If you are interested in developing excellent leadership skills and want to get 'fired up', then read this book!"

—Greg Gerrie author of *Fired Up For Life!*

"The lessons for effective business leadership in *Winning Under Fire* are terrific."

—Mal Bass, President, Executive Forum Group

"Dale Collie reaches into his own impressive background as a U.S. Army Ranger to affirm and confirm how the U.S. Army controls stress and increases productivity with strategies that must work in both planned and unplanned situations. Every reader will find a fit for their own objectives in these real-world Army lessons from Dale. A must-read for every leader."

—Bob Danzig, former CEO, Hearst Newspapers, and author of *There is Only One You*

"A truly tremendous book on my favorite subject. Not the usual clichés, but a book of wisdom written by someone who has walked the talk."

—Charlie (Tremendous) Jones, motivator, publisher, and author of *Life is Tremendous*

". . . an invaluable toolkit of battle-tested stress control strategies and leadership principles that are just as applicable in our business and personal lives."

—Gareth Wood, a leadership development consultant and author of *South Pole: 900 Miles on Foot*

WINNING

UNDER FIRE

★

TURN STRESS

INTO SUCCESS

THE U.S. ARMY WAY

DALE COLLIE

McGraw·Hill

New York   Chicago   San Francisco   Lisbon   London   Madrid   Mexico City
Milan   New Delhi   San Juan   Seoul   Singapore   Sydney   Toronto

Library of Congress Cataloging-in-Publication Data

Collie, Dale.
    Winning under fire : turn stress into success the U.S. Army way / Dale Collie.
       p.   cm.
    Includes index.
    ISBN 0-07-143702-9 (alk. paper)
      1. Job stress.   2. Stress management.   3. Combat—Psychological aspects.
   4. United States Army—Personnel management.   I. Title.

    HF5548.85.C643   2004
    650.1—dc22   2004009320

1 2 3 4 5 6 7 8 9 0   AGM/AGM   3 2 1 0 9 8 7 6 5 4

ISBN 0-07-143702-9

★

Winning Under Fire *is dedicated to all of the heroes who protect American freedom on the battlefront and in the workplace.*

This book is also dedicated to Char Collie, my wonderful wife of thirty-six years, who has encouraged me in every endeavor, and to my parents, Dean and Elsie Collie, who taught me the important things in life.

CONTENTS

INTRODUCTION

As military leaders prepared U.S. forces for combat in Iraq, they anticipated a rapid collapse of the Iraqi army—but they also expected some tough fighting, chemical or biological warfare, and extremely difficult desert conditions. They knew that soldiers would experience severe physical fatigue, uncertainty, and danger, and they also knew that uncontrolled stress could cause as many casualties as could enemy gunfire. Just as Army leaders control stress to avoid battle fatigue and get the best out of their troops, corporate leaders can affect the bottom line by controlling stress to maximize performance and help employees avoid ulcers, heart disease, migraines, and the many other disruptive consequences of negative stress.

Excessive combat stress manifests itself in battle fatigue, and corporate stress can be seen in absenteeism, increased medical costs, lowered productivity, diminished cooperation, and reduced performance. Corporate leaders face challenges similar to the stress of combat as employees deal with everyday crises: demanding corporate goals, high management expectations, departmental confrontations, product failures, customer demands, constant change, and too much work. Both corporate leaders and commanders need the availability of every person to guarantee success; they cannot afford to lose people to the effects of stress.

Army leaders have learned how to keep soldiers on the front line in combat in spite of extreme stress, and good corporate leaders actively incorporate the same leadership, communication, and training strategies to guide the excessive adrenaline and energy into positive results for their companies. Stress control is a leadership responsibility.

Winning Under Fire reveals the Army's well-tested strategies in each of these areas, as well as information from the Army's specially prepared manuals used to train leaders for stress control and combat success. Along with the privileged information about the doctrine of warfare and the operational tools designed for combat, a number of historical and corporate examples in these pages illustrate just how you can use such strategies in the corporate environment. You will also discover the following:

- Techniques used by the Army to control the top ten workplace stressors
- Use of education, training, and after-action reviews (AARs) in reducing stress
- How unit cohesiveness and teamwork help control stress
- Importance of teamwork and the top ten obstacles that get in the way of successful team efforts
- Ten ways to prepare leaders to meet stressors head-on
- Use of the Army's nine principles of war and the Army's five-paragraph field order to control operations and stress
- Value of discipline, practice, resiliency, and surprise in controlling stress
- Six factors of surprise you can use to control stress and retain the upper hand against the competition
- Five common elements of success in major battles and how to apply them for your own success
- Ways you can control your own stress and ensure sound leadership

An elitist saying in the marketplace describes leaders as people who know what must be done and managers as people who handle the details of completing the task. No matter where you find such job descriptions, the wording somehow values the leadership over the management responsibilities. Seldom does the discussion explain that every good manager must also exhibit good leadership characteristics and vice versa—good leadership requires good management skills as well.

Regardless of whether your job description includes the word *leader* or *manager*, you are responsible for the welfare of your company and your people. It is in this context that the words *leader* and *manager* are used interchangeably in *Winning Under Fire*. Keep this in mind as you read through the examples and illustrations, and try to picture the results of properly controlled stress. If these leadership and management skills help Army leaders get the best from their people in military training and combat, their use will surely give you an edge in the marketplace.

1

UNDER FIRE

★

The Vietnamese summer sun was blazing in the afternoon sky when the battalion commander said, "Grab your gear and report to the helipad. You're taking over Delta Company in forty-five minutes. The outgoing commander will brief you on-site." I'd been in the country for only two weeks when I climbed aboard that helicopter loaded with food, ammunition, and mail for this band of 140 young soldiers who had been deployed against the enemy for several months. By the time I stepped from the helicopter onto the dry rice paddy, only an hour of sunlight remained before sundown. As soon as we unloaded the supplies, my predecessor ran past us and jumped into the helicopter as it lifted off the ground. So much for the transition briefing I'd been promised. He was gone, and I was in charge.

The company consisted of three infantry platoons, a mortar platoon, and the command group—three radio operators and me. Since the departing commander had left in such a hurry, one of the radio operators explained the plans to me: the infantry platoons were scheduled to set up ambushes in the surrounding valley, and the command group had plans to spend the night with the mortar platoon in an old French fort nearby. The plans appeared reasonable with some minor adjustments, and staying at the old fort seemed rather clever. It wasn't really a fort but just a waist-high berm of dirt set up as a triangle. Nevertheless, it was a better alternative to digging foxholes on my first day in combat.

Darkness was upon us as we finalized plans, issued orders, and distributed the beans and bullets that came in on the helicopter. As the platoons slipped off into the night, the radio operator notified the battalion of our unit locations. Finally, I could relax with the C-ration can of ham and lima beans that would serve as dinner.

Just as I opened the can, gunfire broke out a few hundred yards to our west, and the radio came alive with a frantic call from the first platoon. "Ambush! Ambush!" they cried. Before I could drop the C-ration can, more gunfire sounded in the opposite direction with a report from the second platoon of enemy contact. Almost immediately the third platoon radioed about an attack on their unit, and even more gunfire erupted. Would we be next?

Even though this was my first real test in battle, I recognized by the timing of the attacks that my location would be the target of the main assault. These other firefights were intended to tie up the line platoons as the Vietcong prepared to attack our command group and the mortar platoon's heavy weapons. Overrunning our command group and capturing the mortars would be a major victory for our opponent.

"Check the machine guns on each corner," I shouted to the mortar platoon leader as we made hasty preparations for the imminent attack on the old fort. We would be very vulnerable if we were not prepared, and firing a machine gun from each corner of the triangular fort was our best chance for survival. The thought crossed my mind that maybe it wasn't such a good idea to stay in this old French fort. But no response came from the mortar platoon leader, so I sent a GI to find him in the darkness. Again and again, I called out to the mortar platoon leader, "Sarge, where are you?"

Even though the sergeant didn't answer, the runner found him sitting with his backside against the wall of dirt. He had both hands on his helmet and his elbows on the ground between his feet when I scrambled over to him. The gunfire had gotten louder at all three locations around us. "Are you wounded, Sarge?" I asked.

"No," came the feeble reply.

"Did you get the machine guns set up, Sarge?" He mumbled a response. "Did you get the guns set up?" I repeated. Again, his response was unintelligible. Grabbing him by the shoulder, I said, "Listen up, Sarge. We're going to be attacked. Help me!"

"I can't, I can't!" cried the sergeant with garbled words and heavy frightened sobs.

"Don't give up on me. You need to get the men ready. You can do it, Sarge," I said urgently. "Just check that machine gun to your right and make sure your guys are spread out along this berm. I'll check over here to the left." As I started away, the frightened sergeant held onto my web gear. I turned to find him standing there in the dark.

He stammered, "I don't know what to tell them, sir."

Pulling him to the ground, I said, "Get down, Sarge, you'll get shot! Go over there by the radios. Stay low." He cowered below the berm of dirt as gunfire from the other platoons echoed through the night.

Mistakes Caused by Stress Can Be Fatal

This was my first gunfight and the Army had trained me well. I knew how to manage the platoons, as I calmly radioed for air support, artillery, and medical evacuations. The collapse of the mortar platoon leader was also something I'd been trained for, but I never expected one of my subordinate leaders to surrender to combat fatigue on my first day in command. The experience, however, prepared me for the future and taught me to anticipate such things, regardless of how established subordinate leaders seem to be.

A hasty analysis revealed that the ambushed platoon was pretty far off of its assigned route. The gunfire was intense, but only the platoon leader was wounded when he threw a baseball-like grenade and then raised his head to see whether it reached the target. This was a dumb mistake for an experienced infantryman who should know that exploding grenades shoot shrapnel just a little farther than most people can throw a grenade.

The ambushed platoon and the others held their own while I continued to prepare for an attack on our position. The radio operator monitoring all of the calls believed that the ambush was real, but he also suspected the other two platoons were shooting at each other. He was right. The platoon leader who had strayed from his assigned route had moved into the path of the third platoon.

When the radio operator anxiously told me of his conclusion, I radioed, "Cease fire! Cease fire!" Strict discipline was required to convince them to quit shooting at each other. As the gunfire between the two *friendly* platoons died off, the enemy also broke contact with the ambushed platoon. Our command position was not attacked, and miraculously, the only person wounded in the whole company was the lieutenant who fragged himself.

A medical evacuation helicopter soon arrived, and the radio operator coordinated the evacuation while I directed our somewhat excited units. "Second and third platoon," I radioed, "Take a head count to make sure you have everyone and then figure out the route to your objective. Continue with your mission."

"Roger, roger," came their subdued, embarrassed replies.

The response from a squad leader in the ambushed platoon was much more enthusiastic when I announced, "You're the acting platoon leader now. Assemble the platoon, take a head count, and watch your rear as you bring them to my position. Your platoon will spend the rest of the night with me."

"Thank you, sir," he responded. His tone of voice made it clear how thankful he was that he would not have complete responsibility for the platoon if they joined the command group.

Why Didn't We Hold Up Under Stress?

The training for all of these soldiers was adequate. The ambushed platoon leader in fact had not strayed off course. He had intentionally chosen the route near the village, a careless error in judgment. Likewise, he had been trained in using grenades and knew that watching the explosion was against all rules of safety. He suffered serious wounds as a result of his inattentiveness.

Years after this combat incident, I encountered similar meltdowns within the first week of my arrival as the new leader of a large organization. The level of stress in the organization before my arrival was so great that the stressfulness of a change in leadership overwhelmed an administrative assistant and a department manager. One hastily resigned, and the other's disruptive attitude created in-house turmoil. The crisis level wasn't very great in either the combat situation or the civilian change of leadership, but the cumulative effect of crises and change overwhelmed those who were already stretched near their capacity.

It is easy to compare the preceding combat incident to corporate accidents since all of the combat errors were actually safety violations. During employment in the chemical industry, I knew of one man who burned to death because he shortcut safety rules regarding the use of a fuel-oil heater to unfreeze a railcar of coal. Another man was almost killed when caught between a truck and the loading dock while acting as a ground guide. A third accident involved a young, conscientious employee who was trying to make up for lost time while operating a forklift truck. The forklift turned over on him, and the recovery period for his crushed pelvis and spinal injuries was similar to that for the inattentive lieutenant who wounded himself with the grenade. Stress was certainly a factor when the lieutenant and the other unfortunate employees suffered from errors in judgment and violations of common safety precautions. Their errors were costly.

All leaders have seen the results of stress overload in highly qualified people, and understanding the dynamics of stress can help leaders deal with those who otherwise perform well. When leaders understand stress, they know why their employees sometimes make careless errors, hold onto illogical arguments, complain endlessly, or suffer from other negative stress reactions. The good news is that when leaders understand the dynamics of stress, they can take action to preclude the consequences of negative stress.

During the previously described night in battle, the ambushed platoon leader caused his own wounds, and the two infantry platoons that engaged each other were fortunate that no one was wounded. A review of the action revealed that the two platoons fired on each other because one of them was way off course. The other platoon thought they had encountered a sizeable enemy force and started shooting.

The navigation failure could have been the result of ignorance, but more likely, it resulted from a reaction to stress—a mental disconnect of some kind that the lieutenant experienced after months of uninterrupted, repetitive stress in pursuit of the enemy. The lieutenant was well trained and very conscientious, but everyone was sleep deprived from running daylight patrols and nighttime ambushes. During these months in the rice paddies and jungles, the poor hygiene was unacceptable for civilized people, and every soldier was emotionally on edge. The threat of enemy contact was always present and casualties were frequent. In short, everyone's stress level ran high.

Another significant contributing factor to the friendly-fire engagement was the silence of the platoon members who recognized that they were way off course. It was later determined that some of the squad leaders and soldiers themselves noted the change of direction but failed to raise the alarm. Some simply thought there had been a change of orders, but others consciously decided to remain silent because they held a grudge against the platoon leader. In retrospect, their silence was illogical, but they too had endured the physical and emotional hardships for months on end, and their poor judgment was a reflection of their own stress levels.

Similar situations can be seen in the corporate world. For example, a manufacturing supervisor I knew in the textile industry once explained that he was so angry about corporate changes that he decided to keep quiet about an impending disaster and let the manager take the blame. When the disaster occurred, the manager was found negligible, but the supervisor's duplicity was discovered, and he was terminated for his failure to take action. With proper stress management, these two good corporate managers could have avoided their difficulties, and the company could have saved the expense of the incident and the personnel replacement costs. A thorough review revealed that the production failure, the poor judgment, and the replacement expenses were actually the result of acute stress caused by management at an even higher level.

The sergeant who froze under the threat of battle is a more poignant example of an acute stress reaction. When he was needed most, his body shut down on him. He had been in combat for a while; this was not his first battle. He was a sergeant, instead of a lieutenant as the command structure prescribed, but he must have demonstrated his ability to handle this very responsible position or he would not have had the assignment. This occurs in business, too: some managers confidently rise up the corporate ladder biting off more than they can chew. These are the ones who freeze in that all-important client meeting or whose ambitions get in the way of managing their own people, even though these managers excelled in every other aspect of their jobs.

In the combat situation, the problems were created by improper leadership. If the people were not properly trained, something should have been done about it prior to the night they fell apart. If these junior leaders were overstressed, action should have been taken to provide relief, individually or as a unit. In corporate work examples, too, leaders are ultimately responsible for the actions of their people, and if the environment is too stressful, the leaders must take action.

The Leader's Responsibility

The near disaster of the *friendly* firefight, the physically wounded lieutenant, and the emotionally damaged sergeant were the price for a lapse in leadership of the outgoing commander, who should have been attentive to the impending stress problems. It would be easy to blame the errors on each of the subordinate leaders, but commanders are ultimately responsible for the success and failure of individuals in their command.

Although I recognize the shortcomings of the previous commander, these failures occurred on *my* watch; I was the one in charge. Since I did not personally know the ability of these platoon leaders, I should have given them assignments to reveal their skill level instead of assuming they were capable just because they were in the leadership positions.

As a leader, it's important to understand that stress can influence anyone's performance, regardless of skill level or experience. Decades of combat have taught the Army to educate all ranks about stress management. If you don't control stress, stress will control you. And this book shows you how to control stress the way the U.S. Army does it.

> "Controlling combat stress is a command responsibility. In terms of service members lost from action and reduced performance, combat stress seriously affects mission accomplishment. It is a leader's responsibility to take action to strengthen service members' tolerance to combat stress and manage it in his or her unit."[1]
>
> **—U.S. Army field manual FM 6-22.5, *Combat Stress***

The first step in controlling stress is to evaluate the stress level in your company. If you are newly appointed to a position of responsibility or if you've just assumed leadership of a company, you'll want to test individuals to make sure they are up to the jobs you expect of them.

If you've been around awhile, you'll want to review how subordinates are doing with their responsibilities. Those experienced people you've trusted might find themselves in over their heads during a time of crisis and on the verge of making costly errors. Routine precautions are inexpensive compared to the mistakes that can result from too much stress. Specific stress management strategies will be discussed in the following chapters.

What Is Stress?

Before examining the effects of stress—both good and bad, consider what is meant by *stress*. The U.S. Army field manual FM 6-22.5, *Combat Stress*, defines combat stress as "the mental, emotional, or physical tension, strain, or distress resulting from exposure to combat and combat-related conditions."

This definition does not preclude other types of stressful situations in the Army, but it takes into account all of the events of warfare as well as those leading up to and supporting the battle—training, readiness, administration, logistics, support, and reserve. Preparation for war can be even more stressful than the actual combat itself. I've heard many U.S. Army Rangers quip that they would rather be in combat than in ranger training. "The only bad thing about combat is the live ammunition," they say. In other words, the stress of training is so great that these soldiers would rather be shot at than return to the school where they learned the art of war.

Compare the Army's definition of stress to the one given by Drs. Lyle Miller and Alma Dell Smith in their bestselling book *The Stress Solution*.[2] Drs. Miller and Smith, leaders in the field of stress research and founding members of the Biobehavioral Institute of Boston and the Biobehavioral Treatment Center, explain that there are three distinct categories of stress: acute, episodic acute, and chronic.

1. **Acute Stress.** This category of stress is significant but temporary, resulting from recent events. Acute stress in small doses can result in positive reactions: the adrenaline rush and feelings of elation can motivate achievement. However, an accumulation of these stressors can have negative effects such as headaches, backaches, upset stomach, and other tension-related responses.

2. **Episodic Acute Stress.** The second category of stress is related to frequently encountered stressors. People experiencing this type of stress are generally overcommitted, lack the time and ability to accomplish everything, and find themselves at odds with coworkers. The consequences of episodic acute stress are much more serious than those in the first category. Irritability turns to anger, occasional tension headaches become frequent migraines, heart palpitations lead to chest pain, and high anxiety becomes a way of life.

3. **Chronic Stress.** The third category is related but carries none of the thrill found with acute stress. The long-term nature of chronic stress is such that people actually become accustomed to the stressors and accept them as a way of life; they see no escape from poverty, job mismatches, abusive situations, or physical hardships.

While stress is much more than a primordial fight-or-flight reaction to threatening situations, the human body does react in complex ways to danger, frustration, anger, and various mental situations. Some of these reactions are favorable in the initial response, as they increase energy, alertness, and stamina so people can respond appropriately to situations. The initial reaction to acute stress, for example, enables people to move faster and think quicker than they normally do. On some occasions of extreme acute stress, such as an impending head-on vehicle accident or other physical danger, a person can think so fast that time seems to stand still while he or she considers the alternatives. The body's response is then amazingly rapid, helping the person avoid the danger.

The well-known hardships of the Army's basic training are certainly stressful, but the favorable response to this stress enables soldiers to accomplish far more than they ever dreamed possible. Corporate managers react in the same positive way as they tackle crisis after crisis to meet manufacturing deadlines, overcome equipment problems, control sales difficulties, and achieve success in spite of seemingly overwhelming odds. Some positive results from acute stress are discussed in the following section.

Stress Causes People to React

According to the Army's *Leaders' Manual for Combat Stress Control,* "stress is the body's and mind's process for dealing with uncertain change and danger. Elimination of stress is both impossible and undesirable in either the Army's combat or peacetime missions."[3] This publication explains the following objectives of stress control:

- To contain stress
- To maximize peak performance and accomplish unit missions
- To return stress levels to normal when they are out of control
- To increase stress tolerance so soldiers can perform under the severe stress situations that are unavoidable in combat

On the other hand, Miller and Smith explain that frequent, ongoing episodes of stress can cause serious health problems and that chronic stress can actually lead to death through suicide or illnesses that result from long-term stress. Everyone is interested in avoiding health problems. People certainly want to help eliminate debilitating chronic stress, but this doesn't mean getting rid of stress altogether.

Corporate employees react the same as soldiers do to sleep deprivation, physical discomfort, irresponsible leadership, and trauma.

Some people are more stress tolerant than others, but everyone has the same type of reactions to these stressful situations.

Tables 1-1 and 1-2 contain the Army's field manual FM 22-51's lists of both mild and severe stress reactions. In the *mild* category are phys-

Table 1-1 Mild Stress Reactions (Physical and Emotional)

1. Anxiety
2. Indecisiveness
3. Irritability
4. Complaining
5. Forgetfulness
6. Inability to concentrate
7. Difficulty thinking, speaking, and communicating
8. Loss of confidence in self and unit
9. Anger
10. Fatigue
11. Dry mouth
12. Pounding heart
13. Insomnia
14. Trembling
15. Jumpiness
16. Cold sweats
17. Nightmares
18. Easily startled by noise, movement, and light
19. Dizziness
20. Tears
21. Crying
22. Nausea, vomiting, or diarrhea
23. "Thousand-yard" stare

The first thirteen *mild* stress reactions listed in Table 1-1 are typical of highly stressed people throughout a wide range of American industries.

ical symptoms such as trembling, cold sweats, dizziness, nausea, and the "thousand-yard stare"—which are pretty severe reactions that one hopes aren't seen often in a corporate environment. But a closer look at the tables reveals many symptoms that people do exhibit on the job: irritability, forgetfulness, and inability to concentrate. Examine the list and see if any of the symptoms have been displayed in your office.

Impulsive reactions such as road rage are a reflection of stress-filled lives. Sometimes, people manifesting many of these symptoms are considered to be simply difficult personalities, but the difficult part of their personality might actually be prompted by high stress on the job or away from the workplace.

Table 1-2 provides symptoms of severe stress that are frequently displayed by such people. Is anyone in your office displaying these issues? If so, they—and you—may have a serious problem.

Employees who experience these severe stress reactions need some immediate relief. Some people won't realize that their stress level is out of control, and they might even deny the need to take action. Tolerating employees who exhibit severe stress reactions isn't doing them a favor. Nor does allowing stress-filled situations to continue help the company. Leaders are responsible for both the detection of these severe stress reactions and for bringing the stress levels back to normal. Later chapters discuss specific practical suggestions for stress management.

The Effects of Stress in the Corporate Setting

Popular opinion says that today's changes in workplace technology, culture, and business management create far more stress for workers than in times past. Just as stress control is a military leadership responsibility, the same applies in corporate leadership. The better that leaders control stress among their people, the better the people will accomplish their missions.

Stress isn't just a day-to-day annoyance. It causes serious problems in the workplace—affecting both employees and the bottom line. The U.S. National Institute for Occupational Safety and Health (NIOSH)

Table 1-2 Severe Stress Reactions (Physical and Emotional)

1. Argumentative nature
2. Reckless action
3. Indifference to danger
4. Memory loss
5. Physical exhaustion
6. Insomnia
7. Rapid emotional shifts
8. Apathy
9. Constant moving around
10. Rapid or inappropriate talk
11. Flinching or ducking at sudden sound and movement
12. Shaking and trembling
13. Inability to use part of body (hand, arm, leg) for no apparent physical reason
14. Inability to see, hear, or feel
15. Severe stutter
16. Mumbling or inability to speak at all
17. Crying
18. Severe nightmares
19. Freezing under fire or total immobility
20. Seeing or hearing things that do not exist
21. Vacant stares
22. Staggering or swaying when standing
23. Panicking and running under fire
24. Social withdrawal
25. Hysterical outbursts
26. Frantic or strange behavior

The first ten severe stress symptoms can also be used to describe overly stressed people in the corporate setting.

reported that stress and related problems are among the most frequent reasons for employee disability. Beyond the positive effects stress can have on productivity, continuous or frequent exposure to stressors creates some seriously negative consequences. The frequent or continuous flow of adrenaline, combined with other physiological reactions to stressors, can become incapacitating.

Northwestern Life Insurance Survey advises that 46 percent of workers reported that their job was very stressful, and even the United Nations reported that job stress has become "the 20th Century Epidemic." In the early nineties, a study by Princeton, New Jersey, insurance company Foster Higgins Co. showed that 60–90 percent of medical problems were associated with stress and that average companies spend about 45 percent of their after-tax profits on health benefits. With the significant increases in health care insurance costs, the price tag for stress-related health claims is much greater today. In his *Harvard Business Review* article "Saving Money by Reducing Stress," A. Perkins[4] presents research showing that 60–90 percent of medical visits are related to stress, but this is just a portion of what stress really costs. The annual cost of corporate stress as it relates to health and productivity costs in America is $50–$150 billion.[5]

If all costs associated with stress-related incidents are considered, the cost per employee is several thousand dollars per year on average. A company can calculate its own costs by determining the cost of absenteeism, accidents, insurance price increases, workers' compensation, reduced productivity, performance errors, customer complaints, and personnel turnover. When management realizes the annual cost of stress, they will see the need to implement stress-reduction programs.

The Army's Balance Between Positive and Negative Stress

In the midst of routine daily duties, good military leaders work hard to strike a balance between the positive stress that encourages high performance and the negative stress that degrades individual or unit capability. The best leaders know how to use positive stress to get the most out of their personnel.

The Army is fanatic about training officers and sergeants to take care of their troops. And these well-trained leaders are fanatic about carrying out their responsibilities. The soldiers in their command don't always realize why these leaders are so focused on having all personnel, equipment, and training 100 percent ready. Even the most personable among these leaders are sometimes accused of managing "by the book" or of being too concerned with their own personal recognition and promotion.

Those who make these allegations, however, miss the point. Just the opposite is true. These "fanatic" leaders are primarily interested in the welfare of their troops and in carrying out their unit mission. Strict discipline, intensive and complete training, and numerous inspections are essential for combat readiness. Failing to enforce regulations, conduct detailed inspections, or practice combat readiness is tantamount to dereliction of duty. The extra effort that goes into intensive training programs creates additional stress in the unit, but less persistent commanders actually endanger their troops and their mission when they fail to schedule training that teaches troops how to deal with stress.

Detecting Stress

Some corporate jobs are just as stressful as military assignments, and some ongoing business situations are as stressful as armed combat. You can find the stressed employees by monitoring the frequency of the conditions shown in Tables 1-1 and 1-2.

Privacy laws preclude corporate managers from knowing all about their employees' reasons for medical assistance, but the following are practical ways to determine what is going on in your organization:

- Require strict reporting of absences. Watch for changes or trends; the more absenteeism, the greater the chance that stress is a factor.

- Develop a report on tardiness. Are some departments worse than others? Are people arriving late because they dread the upcoming stress?
- Seek generic information from your health insurance company on the number and expense of medical claims. Categorize information by type of ailment and observe how the frequency of visits compares to major corporate activities or stressful times of year. You might find that stressful periods coincide with or precede an increase in medical claims.
- Get professional assistance in analyzing how stress might be at the root of physical ailments. The experts might recognize cause-and-effect relationships that escape the attention of those who aren't as well trained in stress control.
- Keep a record of complaints or grievances filed by department. Those departments that have greater numbers of complaints are likely ready for some stress-control strategies.
- Analyze accident reports from the perspective of stress involvement. Research how stress might have been the root cause of accidents.
- Develop a way to log errors in judgment or misstatements. This will help you evaluate the cost of stress for your company.
- Note changes in the way people relate to each other and the types of action that cause some people to become more argumentative at times. You can use this information to control stress for the entire organization or for specific individuals who are more sensitive to stressful situations.
- Review customer service problems from a stress perspective. Determine whether some kind of stress reduction could improve relations with customers or reduce the number of errors involved with order taking, preparation, shipping, or invoicing.

An understanding of positive stress is needed to maximize accuracy and productivity, but not all leaders are taught to manage stress or to observe for negative stress reactions. If qualified staff is available, it would be profitable to train all leaders and managers in the basics of stress management from a corporate perspective. Outside consultants and trainers are also available to assist with this important aspect of leadership.

> Corporate leaders and managers sometimes try to manage the stressed *people* by using increased demands and closer supervision. Instead, you should use stress-reducing techniques to manage the *stressors*.

It is important to manage employees and to help them understand how to manage their individual stress, but if you're interested in maximizing your company's productivity, you'll also want to learn how leaders and managers can take part in the improvement. What changes can be made in companies to alleviate *unnecessary* stressors?

While the demanding remedies of dictatorial managers might get short-term improvement from stressed employees, such relief is usually only temporary. The increased urgency and focus on details typically generates even more stress, and the problems shift from slight distractions, such as back pain, headaches, and inattention, to more drastic reactions such as absenteeism and medical problems, both good indicators that stress levels need attention.

How About Your Organization?

The importance of mission readiness is just as great across corporate America as it is in the military. The bottom-line costs in terms of net profits, missed opportunities, and personnel turmoil are good enough reasons to emphasize stress control, and proper stress control can contribute to business growth and job security for everyone involved.

If you want to fulfill your own responsibilities as a leader, you'll want to ask some tough questions about your own organization:

- Are there stressful situations in your organization that need attention?
- Are some people pushed too hard by corporate demands, family situations, or medical problems?

- Are some people unaware of the seriousness of their situation, and do they need professional attention?
- Will your company pay a price for not attending to these individual stress cases, or will it improve by giving attention to the stressors that affect each employee?

The chapters in this book contain information on how to prevent, manage, and control the stress that can drastically affect your entire organization. You'll learn how to create environments conducive to error-free performance. You'll also learn that if employees get in trouble because of bad attitudes, you need to take into account reasons for that action before handing out punishment.

Whether the stressors are within your company or outside the company's control, everyone is better served if an effort is made to compensate for the stress. You'll learn how to control your own stress as well as that of employees, and you'll find out how the Army controls stress during combat. Adapting these strategies to the corporate way of life can benefit personal lives and the bottom line.

What About the Stressed-Out Leaders from the Old French Fort?

For years I thought that the soldiers at the old French fort had intentionally disobeyed orders or were simply unprepared for combat. Later, I realized that their training had indeed carried them through several months of combat, but they were eventually overwhelmed by the sustained stress of continuous combat operations. Both their thought process and performance were affected by long periods of strenuous physical conditions in leech-infested rice paddies and jungles, frequent contact with the enemy, poor nutrition, sleep deprivation, and loss of friends through combat wounds and normal reassignment to the United States.

My first day in combat coincided with their crises, and we were fortunate not to have confronted a well-organized enemy force. The platoon leaders made some errors, but they were doing their best with what they knew and the tools they had available to them. The same goes for my own leadership, but through all of these events, I learned valuable lessons to apply in my military career and in business.

You might be experiencing a similar crisis in your company. The remaining chapters illustrate how you can apply some tried-and-true techniques.

Notes

1. U.S. Army field manual FM 6-22.5, *Combat Stress*, Headquarters, Department of the Army, Washington, D.C., June 23, 2000.
2. Drs. Lyle Miller and Alma Dell Smith, *The Stress Solution: An Action Plan to Manage the Stress in Your Life*, March 1993. Published by Pocket Star.
3. U.S. Army field manual FM 22-51, *Leaders' Manual for Combat Stress Control*, Headquarters, Department of the Army, Washington, D.C., September 29, 1994, paragraph 1-2d.
4. A. Perkins, "Saving Money by Reducing Stress," *Harvard Business Review*, 1994, 72(6): 12.
5. S. L. Sauter, et al., "Prevention of Work-Related Psychological Disorders," *American Psychologist*, 45(10): 1146–1153.

2

STRESS TRIGGERS

★

When new soldiers arrive for basic training, they are met by drill ser geants who are specialists at increasing stress. The stern orders and directives might seem like harassment to the poor teenagers who seem unable to do anything right. No matter how hard they try, it is never good enough.

The high stress, however, is intentional and part of the training. While there might be some negative reactions, the purpose is to help these soldiers achieve far more than they would ever expect. Drill sergeants know when to coach, when to instruct, when to raise the temperature, and when to use compassion to relieve the stress. By the time recruits graduate from basic training, they admire and respect these tyrants who manipulate the recruits' stress to help them achieve.

The stress found in regular units isn't usually as dramatic as the confrontations with the drill sergeants, but the continued training, equipment maintenance, record keeping, and readiness inspections keep stress at very high levels. Even when war seems unlikely, soldiers continually prepare for wartime. Every unit trains for and is constantly evaluated on their combat readiness. Throughout the year, combat units practice for and often are tested on their individual and unit skills at all levels—squad, platoon, company, and battalion.

The combatlike training prepares soldiers for battle. Tanks roll across difficult terrain and fire their cannons in simulated combat. Pilots are challenged with real and simulated operations in support of ground forces. Artillery troops prepare their big guns and practice both live fire and the maneuvers required to keep up with the forward units. Soldiers have very little time to relax properly, and families feel the strain of Army life in the soldiers' long work hours and frequent absences.

Corporate leaders can identify with the soldiers' plight. Few businesses experience the roar of cannon fire, but almost every corporate manager has known the stress of demanding business conditions and the roar of a dissatisfied boss.

Preparing for Stress

The stress triggers of combat seem obvious, but to the uninitiated, it is difficult to explain just how stressful things can be for soldiers in the peacetime training and unit maintenance environment. When soldiers get ready for battle, stress control is so important that trained stress specialists consult with commanders to monitor and control stress levels for both soldiers and their families. Knowing that family members are well cared for is a big relief for combat soldiers, so every unit is charged with establishing family support groups to help with every concern. These efforts help control stress among deployed soldiers and help families deal with their soldier's absence.

As soldiers prepared for war in Iraq, for example, conscientious efforts were made to balance stress control with combat readiness. None of the leaders had to create a positive stress environment to maximize preparation, but the officers and key sergeants knew they had to control the mounting stress to minimize the negative reactions among those awaiting deployment.

To help control stress, soldiers were informed of their combat mission and how long they might expect to be away from home, what their working and living conditions would be like, and details about the enemy. Families were informed of what could be expected at home and in Iraq. Additional medical care was provided to all family members to take care of lingering problems. Legal assistance was provided to inform everyone about wills, powers of attorney, and other matters that could be distracting to soldiers and their families after deployment. Financial counseling was made available for anyone who needed to open or close bank accounts or get additional names on signature cards. Whenever possible, soldiers were given additional time off to be with their families. Family counseling was provided to prepare everyone for the soldier's departure, their absence, and their eventual return. Chaplains made every effort to prepare and encourage those who needed spiritual direction.

Some people cope well with all of these stressors and some don't. Many see the circumstances as difficult and inconvenient, but others who are just as dedicated become overwhelmed and see the situation as impossible. Therefore, anticipating reactions to stress is important. If stress is prevented or minimized, soldiers enter into situations with a better attitude that is geared more for success. Before learning how to minimize stress, it's important to understand what can trigger stress.

> The thing that keeps soldiers going is their attitude toward all the different types of stressors they encounter.

What's Causing All of This Stress?

Stressors come from internal and external sources, both in the military and the corporate arenas. Internal stressors are things like illness, improper nutrition, inadequate rest, bad attitudes, and so on. External physical stressors, of course, come from outside the body and might be categorized as the following:

- **Sensory overload**—extremes in temperature, humidity (wet or dry), noise, odors, other physical discomforts
- **Imbalance of relationships**—interpersonal communications, criticism, friendships, supervisory contact

- **Imbalance of expectations**—workload, deadlines, appearance, skills, talents, desires

In the workplace, the terms *internal* and *external* stress have additional definitions. Internal corporate stressors come from inside the company, such as deadlines, hostile coworkers, or demanding clients. External corporate stressors are those the company cannot control, like the family dog getting run over, children are not performing well in school, illness of an extended family member, tax season, or a failing marriage. The following sections look more carefully at these internal and external workplace stressors to fully clarify their impact on performance.

Stress Triggers Unrelated to Work

The stress caused by day-to-day living is frequent and has a great impact on people. Some of the stress is positive, encouraging accomplishment, but an accumulation of this type of stress has a negative effect on the body's systems. Heavy traffic, construction delays, dented fenders, and tire problems are pretty strong triggers. A hot day, a phone call with bad news, unexpected bills, house repairs, family problems, and bad weather are all triggers that raise people's stress levels. Toothaches, athlete's foot, hangnails, blisters, eye infections, earaches, and other routine ailments can add to your level of stress. Major illnesses and diseases can almost max out the stress scale, as can constant or chronic pain from a variety of sources. And don't forget the stress accompanying the responsibility of taking care of your immediate and extended family or aging parents and their needs. Whether you are in a position to help those with special needs or you simply are aware of the situations, they bring a good deal of added stress.

Even if everything is pretty much under control in your own life, you can't escape external stress, because the news media and entertainment industry do all they can to feed the stress engines of America. If there are no tragedies in your city or community, the media reaches across the United States and the world to bring you news of some terrible incident. Instead of bringing us tranquility, the world of entertainment has also developed a special talent for showing realistic violence and mayhem. In short, stress comes from everywhere in the external world.

Work-Related Stress Triggers

Stress triggers in the workplace are just as numerous as the external triggers. Stressors include bosses, deadlines, coworkers, customers, production, service, product management, accounting problems, computer services, engineering concerns, sales, marketing, advertising, public relations, human resources, stockholders, legal issues, and distribution. Every department causes stress for itself and for others.

No matter where you are in the corporate hierarchy, you are subject to stress from every department and person with whom you come in contact. Everyone else has the same kinds of concerns as you do. In trying to accomplish their own work, they'll find themselves in conflict with others who have their own agendas. Those customers who keep calling with special needs really get in the way of completing the boss's assignment on time. Couple all of this with payroll errors and medical insurance claims that weren't handled properly, and you have a day filled with stress triggers—and stress reactions.

Typically, a combination of stress triggers work together to create reactions far beyond what is deserved by any single stressor. When the family dog is sick and your daughter is upset about an incident at school, the traffic delays and poor drivers combine to make a stressful beginning of a workday. An overly anxious boss who gives you very short notice for a report adds to the level of stress.

> The Army teaches leaders to "Know your troops, and be alert for any sudden, persistent or progressive change in their behavior that threatens the functioning and safety of your unit."
>
> **—Army field manual FM 6-22.5, *Combat Stress***

Added to this are layers of situations that increase stress. Customers threaten to change suppliers, vendors announce price increases, employees leave for better opportunities, and good employees are discharged because of the shifting marketplace. Almost every situation in business is a stress trigger and almost every situation before and after the business day brings stress of its own.

Most Stress Is Unnecessary

The impact of specific stressors is determined by the total amount of stress a person is experiencing. What might be considered a small irritant on one occasion might be the straw that broke the camel's back on another.

While businesses can't control all external stressors, action can be taken to minimize internal stressors such as the following:

- Unreasonable expectations for greater productivity, manufacturing or administrative
- Positioning people in jobs that do not use skills and abilities
- Underpaying for the level of responsibility assigned to individuals
- Vague and arbitrary promotion policies
- Management's failure to consider employees' perspectives in decisions affecting their jobs
- Excessive overtime with or without compensation
- Arbitrary assignment of unpleasant tasks
- Failure to enforce policies for some individuals
- Poor top-down and bottom-up communications procedures
- Poor problem-solving strategies or mediation of conflicts between employees
- Family separation, through transfers or frequent business trips
- Demonstrated lack of concern for employees' welfare
- Intolerable environmental conditions—temperature, hazardous, noise, light, odors, and so on

Just as corporate leaders are responsible for maximizing performance and increasing net profits, they are also responsible for controlling stressors that can affect the bottom line. It is difficult to remove some of these stressors when a company is under attack by the competition or suffering from adverse economic conditions, but this challenge is just as important as any other skill set of those who wear the mantle of leadership.

Controlling Stress at the First Sign

Frontline leaders are taught to control stress in their units rather than evacuate soldiers at the first sign of *battle fatigue*, the Army's name for negative reactions to acute stress. The negative stress reactions of battle are considered normal, even though they can be pretty severe, going well beyond the tension headache. Soldiers can still function in spite of flinching, shaking, physical exhaustion, rapid emotional shifts, and other manifestations of extreme stress.

Experience shows that coaching, confidence building, food, and rest help overcome most of the negative stress reactions of battle fatigue. Just as important is the understanding that soldiers treated near the front line recover much faster than soldiers evacuated to rear-area hospitals for essentially the same treatment.

Serious cases and those who do not respond to frontline treatment are evacuated, however, and cared for by specially trained psychiatrists and psychologists in rear-area hospitals where medical facilities are staffed for such circumstances.

For severe cases of stress, you, too, will want assistance from professional counselors. Many companies have contracts for professional care through their health care programs and refer employees who manifest serious signs of stress. However, just as military leaders strive to control stress, corporate leaders can be trained to help overstressed employees on the front line and maintain employees on the job. The frontline actions are just as likely to succeed in a business as they are in combat. See Chapter 9 for details on how Army leaders are trained to control stress in their units.

Some external stressors, such as incapacitated relatives who must have the full-time assistance of the service member, are far from the reach of the military leader, but if they seriously affect accomplishing the unit mission, decisions will have to be made about whether the service member can remain on active duty.

Six Steps in Treating Combat Stress Reactions

1. Reassurance
2. Rest and sleep
3. Food and fluids
4. Hygiene—washing up with warm or cool water as needed, putting on clean uniform
5. A chance to talk about what happened
6. Restoring the soldier's identity and confidence with useful work

In addition to these six steps, Army field manual FM 22-51, *Leaders' Manual for Combat Stress Control*, explains that "Treatment should be administered as quickly, as simply, and as close to the soldier's unit as possible."

In addition to controlling internal stressors, the Army uses many other methods to alleviate external stressors (e.g., medical, psychological, family counseling, spiritual, special education, social services, etc.), all of which can be used for special family situations. In some cases, however, the stress reaction is manifested in low productivity or inappropriate actions (misconduct or illegal activities), and soldiers sometimes face legal repercussions or separation from the Army. When stress leads to the excessive use of alcohol or the use of illegal drugs, for example, the consequences are severe.

These instances are few in comparison to the thousands of situations resolved through command attention. Leaders deal with situations as they develop, as close to the front line as possible, with emphasis on keeping the soldier in place to accomplish the unit's mission. The same can be done in the corporate environment.

Stress in Action—an Example

To understand how business leaders can use military procedures to deal with external stressors, consider one of the greatest external stressors for both the Army and most corporations: family situations.

When it comes to controlling the impact stressors have on the accomplishment of the unit mission, the Army views family-related stress just as they do the internal, militarily generated situations. If a personal problem affects the mission, the Army leader must take action to control its impact.

Although the family might never see the inside of the corporate workplace, they certainly have an impact on corporate productivity and profits. It isn't unusual for employees to ask for time off to get medical attention for their children. Others repeatedly ask to leave work early to help a spouse with car problems or other minor crises. You get the picture. Some families are high maintenance. When sorting through personal problems of employees, you might find the following Army system useful:

- Confront the problem as a frontline situation.
- Make an effort to keep employees in service instead of developing a scenario for their replacement.
- Offer professional assistance.
- Let the employees be a part of the solution.

Here's an example of how this practice works in a corporate setting. I once had an employee whose child had a weak immune system, and he frequently asked for time off because the day care center wouldn't care for sick children. Some kind of issue came up every week. When he was absent, other employees had to cover his responsibilities, and I found myself filling in more often than I liked.

When I confronted the employee, he was distressed about his child's health as well as his wife's inability to help in this situation. "Why can't your wife share some of this responsibility?" I asked.

"Oh, she wants to, but her company won't let her have time off."

I gave the employee two weeks to find an alternative plan, because we truly needed him at the office. "I really care about your child's health," I told him. "But I need a full forty hours a week from you. If we could get by with less, we would hire a part-time person.

"I don't mind if you take off from time to time, and there might be a way to do some flexible scheduling if that would help your family situation. If you want some professional assistance in developing a solution, I'll give you some numbers to contact. You might even propose other ways to overcome the problem.

"Whatever you come up with, we want you to plan a full week at the office, every week, starting two weeks from today. In the meantime, do what is needed to keep things together in your family. All of you are important to us."

During the following two weeks, the employee discussed alternatives on three occasions. Then the family decided to find another day care center that could handle their child's needs. They had some emotional attachment to the first day care center, but in the end, they made the choices necessary to accomplish their family objectives while meeting the attendance requirements of both employers.

Morale in the office increased, and the employee felt better about his productivity. He never left the office again because of day care problems. His family was stronger and happier with the new day care arrangement. Eventually, he became the number two manager in the office, well on his way to making a career with the company.

This problem could have been handled with an admonishment or a warning letter. We could have threatened him with the consequences of his continued behavior. Instead, I made it clear that I was concerned about his family, emphasizing how much his presence meant to the office team. He appreciated our offer to help, but he resolved the situation on his own. This family stress problem had a happy ending because I used the preceding Army strategy.

Of course, not all external family stressors are obvious to military or corporate leaders. Most leaders will never know of family arguments, teenage rebellion, in-law squabbles, or cantankerous spouses. If productivity isn't what it should be, or if there are unexplained signs of stress, it is time for some one-on-one counseling to find out what is at the root of the problem.

Initial Relief of Major Stress Triggers

Extended absences or long hours at the office can also cause negative stress reactions among employees and their families. This is another example where corporate managers can influence external stressors to avoid damage to the bottom line. Anything done to reduce stress at home will have an impact on productivity and efficiency at work. The following suggestions, which are based on techniques used by the U.S. Army, show how you can reduce stress in employee households:

• Provide corporate newsletters with detailed information about the company and special projects. The Army has had great success in communicating through informal unit newsletters. The more families know about the company, the better they can support their family-member–employee. Families probably don't care about the financial information found in a prospectus, but they do care about products, marketing efforts, success in the marketplace, working conditions, benefits and alternatives, referral information for professional services, stories about other employees, birthdays, anniversaries, and weddings. Personal recognition in letters can overcome a significant amount of stress.

• Provide corporate communications about the use of company benefits (e.g., insurance, credit unions, banking facilities, entertainment opportunities, and industry news). No matter how much a company thinks employees understand the benefit packages, this type of information needs to be included in family communications.

• Plan social functions for small teams, departments, divisions, and corporate personnel. Leaders can be socially engaging or the corporation can plan discounted group travel and entertainment activities. Employees and families accept these events much better if they are scheduled as part of ongoing relationships and trust-building efforts rather than something sponsored during the employee's absence.

• Offer compensatory time, which is useful to help families get reacquainted and to help employees accomplish the many tasks that go uncompleted during an extended absence. Bonus vacation schedules can be stress relievers if the workload is shared in such a way that the vacation doesn't simply delay the employee's work that must be done. Extra time off is a good stress reliever for family separations caused by time or distance. You might reward individuals with what the Army calls a three-day pass to be used when it is meaningful to the family. The resulting increased productivity will more than make up for any lost time on the job.

• After extended absences orientations and information about family reunions, are beneficial because such reunions can be stressful after extended absences. Many returning employees are left out of important decisions that they once controlled, and few admit their true feelings about the stay-at-home member's taking responsibility for many things the employee would normally do. Returning employees upset the normal functioning of the family when they try to resume the helm and want to counter various procedures established in their absence. Corporate seminars or counseling can be useful in helping everyone understand the dynamics of changed routines and decision-making.

• Have complaint–information desks, which can be helpful to spouses and families who do not have the resources to get answers or tackle problems. The information desk or ombudsman doesn't solve problems, but does point the family member in the right direction for things such as payroll errors, expense reimbursement, medical claims, communications with the employee, and rumor control.

• Set up referral desks that can help management determine which areas of operation need attention, which are providing inadequate information or training, and which require additional training in interpersonal skills. The ombudsman can receive, categorize, and report complaints while helping people solve problems.

Vacations as Stress Relievers

Most employed Americans look forward to their annual vacations, but companies don't always see the increased productivity and stress relief they hope to achieve with these paid absences. Instead of finding vacations relaxing, many families find them to be very stressful times. The planning, packing, prodding, and expense can be overwhelming. It has been said often, and only half jokingly, "I had to come back to work to rest up."

Modern vacations might even be more stressful than those of the past if flights or highway travel is involved. And all of this is just to get to the destination, where more stress awaits the vacationer. Whether going to a resort or to visit extended family, the new environment is often more stressful than staying home.

Developing a process to relieve the stress of vacation is one of the best things you can do to maximize your company's significant investment in this annual ritual. Here are fourteen things you can do to help your people to return from vacation well rested, full of enthusiasm, and stress free.

1. **Avoid announcing job changes or new responsibilities just before employees leave for vacation.** The amount of work they get done on the new project before the vacation is minimal. Their expectations and concerns will fluctuate during their absence, and they'll have no one to talk with about their concerns. Wait until they return to break the good news.

2. **Make frequent announcements about ways to save money for vacations, and make sure banks or credit unions can help employees budget for this large annual expense.** It's easy to overestimate how much employees know about simple financial management. Announcements and special arrangements help them plan while also demonstrating your concern—good relationship-building and stress-reducing opportunities. Your company bank or credit union might follow the lead of the financial institutions that help the Army with these plans and announcements.

3. **Provide credit and budget counseling to help employees avoid overwhelming expenses.** Some people who initially give attention to this type of counseling for vacation purposes find the effort very beneficial in other ways. Many adopt permanent savings strategies for education and retirement. Others find ways to reduce debt. This type of counseling is prevalent in the Army as commanders assume per-

sonal responsibility for making sure soldiers pay their bills and budget their income. No soldier wants a commander to receive creditor complaints about money they owe.

4. **Have the payroll department double-check disbursements for errors to make sure there are no last-minute glitches in the employee paycheck or direct deposit.** Even if payroll has an excellent record, double-checking these records is worthwhile. The one error a year could come on an employee's paycheck while he or she is traveling and unable to confirm the transaction. Dealing with bounced checks or overdrawn credit cards while on vacation is no way to reduce stress. If payroll is unwilling to verify everyone before their vacation, maybe you can get them to at least verify your team members. The numerous changes that occur within corporate payrolls create many opportunities for errors.

5. **Consider distributing job responsibilities among other team members during employees' absences so they don't return to an overflowing inbox.** Just imagine what it would be like to return to your own desk after vacation and find an empty in-box. What a relief it would be to find out that someone else had taken care of all the urgent matters and that the routine paperwork would be available after you have taken care of important e-mail and voice mail. You can help yourself and your employees by teaching them how to use filters and mailboxes to sort and prioritize incoming e-mail messages. Treat this administrative work just as you would any other part of your teamwork, and let the team help with the details just as the Army would in combat.

6. **Provide in-house orientations on how to organize a stress-free vacation.** Don't assume that everyone is as skilled as you are in planning vacations. Sometimes executives use agents and travel planners for their own vacations and forget that many people have to do all that work themselves. Workshops or assistance from corporate staff would be very meaningful for employees of all levels. The Army's Recreational Services branch provides this kind of service. Consider finding a travel agent who will fill this same role.

7. **Negotiate some preplanned vacation packages for your employees.** Many travel agencies have three- to five-day packages and longer that they can customize for your employees. Refer employees to specific travel agents who can assist with planning and expenses. The discounts available to you as a company and the added travel business can score points with both employees and the travel planners. The Army handles this quite successfully through the Army–Air Force Exchange System with domestic and international tours that they contract with civilian travel agencies. Corporations can work with the agency that handles their corporate travel or one of the well-established travel clubs.

8. **Let everyone know the best ways to research travel expenses on the Internet**—for example, reliable discount websites for travel, accommodations, and destinations. It would be worth your efforts to see whether you can negotiate additional discounts for company employees. This is another great opportunity to provide a free seminar. Be sure to invite family members.

9. **Allow an extra half-day or full day to prepare for the vacation**—for example, house and pet arrangements, servicing cars and buying tires, purchasing luggage and special apparel, making arrangements for children. These distractions are very likely going to consume a good part of the employee's last day at the office anyway. The expense to the company is negligible compared with the benefit to the employee. Large corporations might find some middle ground on this subject to get the benefit of giving extra time off without fracturing the company's finances.

10. **Counsel individuals two weeks before the vacation to make sure they get those company priorities out of the way.** Check up on this. Ask them to tell you what must be done, and then monitor their efforts. They don't need their last day at work filled with nerve-wracking deadlines. Not all Army leaders take advantage of this, but those who have developed a caring relationship with soldiers in their command use this technique to relieve the stress of getting ready for vacation.

11. **Plan for the return of employees by scheduling a time to discuss their vacation (relationship building) and to catch them up on what has transpired during their absence.** Keep a log of things you'll tell them about so you'll have a meaningful discussion—something more than "everything went as usual." If you work side by side with employees, this communication can be a part of your daily conversation. Either way, employees will be impressed with your personal interest and the fact that you stopped to catch up on things that are important to their families. This type of debriefing is enhanced by the Army's vertical management structure that limits the number of soldiers reporting to a single leader. If your corporate structure is flatter, with many employees reporting to a single manager, you might designate some team leaders who can adapt this strategy.

12. **If you know the employee's destination and have emergency contact information, do something special** like sending their family a note to be delivered to their room, or a postcard, flowers, or fruit basket. This is a home-run relationship builder, family trust builder, and stress reliever. If your budget is as limited as the Army's, the personal note is a very effective approach.

13. **Communicate with employees when establishing vacation schedules.** Many companies used to shut down for a specified vacation period rather than deal with the complex schedules and cross-training required to keep things running while key people are on vacation. Some still use this practice, but the companies who are flexible in allowing employees to choose their vacation period find the process much better in relieving stress and rejuvenating employees. The Army permits individuals to apply for personal leave (vacation) whenever they choose, and permission is granted based upon mission performance and scheduled events.

14. **Require vacation periods of one or two weeks for high-stress jobs versus allowing one- to two-day segments as many prefer.** My personal experience in high-pressure jobs is that one week is required for me to leave the job behind and relax, and the second week is necessary to rest up for my return. Remember, the purpose

of vacation is twofold: (1) to benefit the individuals and (2) to improve their performance at the company. Since the company is paying for this break, it needs to be structured to benefit everyone concerned. Just as in the Army, it is tempting to allow key personnel to skip their vacation entirely when the workload is significant, but the rewards are much greater if people are required to adhere to the vacation schedule.

Minimizing Stress Triggers

Corporate leaders have a lot of influence over both internal and external stress triggers. Leaders who are concerned about employee well-being easily implement measures to control stress reactions, and those who are concerned only about net profits can see the benefit of controlling stress to improve corporate performance. Just as people try to minimize negative stress reactions, they use positive stress situations in an effort to get better results. The positive aspects are discussed in more detail in Chapter 3.

3

THE STRESS EDGE

★

What's So Positive About Positive Stress?

Some stress is a good thing. People need stress to reach goals, get things done on time, take care of personal needs, and protect themselves. When danger approaches or when a person is confronted by a high-stress situation, a special part of the brain's hypothalamic-pituitary-adrenal (HPA) system tells the body to produce steroid hormones, which flow throughout the body and get the systems ready for action. Major organs, such as the heart, lungs, liver, and kidneys, play a role in stress reaction. The systems controlled by these organs also get a jump start—for example, the metabolism, the digestive system, the immune system, and the circulatory system. Even the skin gets involved by reacting to changes in the circulatory and immune systems.

The HPA system also releases neurotransmitters and tells parts of the brain to go into overdrive. A particular part of the brain creates the emotional response of fear in the case of danger, and another part of the brain stores the event in long-term memory for future warning. One of the neurotransmitters can actually shut down short-term memory and diminish a person's ability to concentrate. Logical and rational thought can be affected, and inhibitions reduced.

In the case of fear or high anxiety, rapid breathing provides more oxygen to the body, and more red and white blood cells are produced. An increased heart rate carries more blood cells and oxygen to all organs; the body is getting ready for action.

And that isn't all that's happening. When a person's anxiety level is up, the immune system reroutes infection fighters to the skin and other vital places, and fluids and blood are rerouted from nonessential areas. This is why the mouth gets dry and the skin takes on an unusual color—sometimes making a person "pale as a ghost." If fright ever caused your hair to stand on end, it was the result of your scalp tightening with the rerouting of blood. And the digestive system shuts down during periods of high anxiety; that's why a person doesn't feel like eating just before giving a speech or interviewing for a new job.

The body's rapid reaction to stress is complex as a person confronts and overcomes obstacles throughout the day. The stressor doesn't have to be life-threatening to get a physical reaction. Something as non-threatening as making a cold call on a customer or starting up an operating line can trigger the whole series of stress reactions.

The same mental and physical responses just described occur when soldiers encounter stressful situations. Even during periods of mild stress, commanders have to remind troops to drink more water and to eat when situations permit. Because of the neurotransmitters released by the HPA system, extremely stressed soldiers are unable to remember some of the events that should be stored in short-term memory, which also explains why different people remember different parts of a stressful event or remember actions in different ways.

Using Positive Responses

Command assignments, realistic training, and combat experience increased my own ability to react properly in periods of high stress and taught me to use the rush of adrenaline to get the job done. Whenever I recognized anxiety and danger, I embraced the emotional shift and channeled it into excitement and energy rather than fear and worry. Soldiers sometimes are unaware of the complex systems of stress response, but they know that a controlled response brings with it an increase in energy, sensory awareness, strength, and stamina.

The Army starts teaching this response to new soldiers when they arrive at the U.S. Army Reception Station. The entire process is set up to shock their systems and create as much stress as possible. The arrival is typically at a late hour. The scene is shocking in its stark military appearance. Sergeants are yelling at the recruits before they even have a chance to respond. Hair is shaved. Uniforms are thrust at the new soldiers. And orders are issued in such a way that no one can complete what is demanded of them.

The stressful approach is calculated to get these new soldiers to perform at levels they never dreamed possible. These first few weeks of stress pay off as the training is burned into their brains for future use. A change in metabolism brings down their weight, and increased exercise strengthens their muscles. These positive stress reactions prepare soldiers to achieve more and learn faster as they gain confidence in themselves. And as the next section points out, corporate leaders can use this kind of positive stress reaction.

Positive Stress and Corporate Life

Most companies use varying levels of this positive stress strategy. Managers confront salespeople with ever-increasing sales targets. Production managers must constantly lower costs and increase production. Customer service levels are never high enough to suit management. Ever-changing laws and regulations keep finance and accounting departments on their toes. Those who are affected by such leadership strategies don't always see the stress as positive; nevertheless they are motivated to action and are given the physical, mental, and emotional readiness to deal with the stressful situations.

No one wants to face the threat of losing a job, but such a stressor can provide a motivation to do the necessary actions to keep the job. Having a positive attitude is key. For example, the reaction to the threat of a job loss can be channeled into acquiring additional training to improve performance, getting assistance from other people, or even preparing for a voluntary job change. People with negative attitudes might react by decreasing performance or becoming argumentative. It is easy to see how the negative reactions could lead to even greater stress without any future benefit.

As the stress level increases, people's brains and bodies benefit from their reactions to threatening situations. People are equipped for action, but they have to decide how to use all the extra energy. Will you work harder to get the big sale, or will you use the stress as an excuse for avoiding the phone calls and effort needed to achieve?

Using Stress to Succeed

To maximize productivity, leaders must understand how to encourage stress at the right time and when to minimize stress to prevent negative stress reactions. Stressful events have tempered everyone, making some people more capable when performing under stress. Those who have not been prepared properly often fold under pressure and give a terrible performance.

Take, for example, a salesclerk who has lost the paperwork for an urgently needed order. The clerk is embarrassed that he has lost the order and readily admits his error. When asked why he didn't call the customer to reconstruct the order, he replies, "I was afraid the customer would be mad."

The stress of the lost documents was overwhelming for the clerk. His short-term, logical thought process obscured the ultimate consequences of his actions. He couldn't see that everyone would be more understanding of his early admission and reorder of the products than they would be with his waiting until it was too late to complete the order at all. There is a chance that good leadership can improve the clerk's performance, but he might leave the job if he is unable or unwilling to build his stress tolerance.

Whatever their level of responsibility, those who react illogically have either suffered acute stress for a long while, or they have never been trained to use stress in a positive way. For reasons they don't understand, they avoid seeking assistance with the situation, getting additional training, or even trying to work through the stressful process.

This type of reaction can, however, be turned around. For example, professional salespeople take the stress of frequent rejections and use its added energy to find alternatives. Instead of caving in to the stress, they use it to their advantage. These people will always encounter stress, so channeling their stress reactions is advantageous. You can help people increase their stress tolerance and learn to channel fear into positive reactions by repeatedly exposing them to stressful situations while coaching, encouraging, and demonstrating positive stress reactions.

George S. Patton and a Pocket Notebook

If you know how your body will react under stress, you can prepare for it. I learned this lesson at one point in my Army career, when I was the aide-de-camp for Major General George S. Patton Jr., the son of the famous World War II general. I'd worked with several high-ranking officers, but that first day on the job with General Patton was right at the top of the high-stress scale.

When General Patton came through the door, he met my cheery greeting with a gruff, "Come in here, Collie." As I stood before his desk, General Patton gave me three simple projects to complete.

When I turned to leave, he said, "Come back here, Collie. Tell me what you're going to do." After I repeated the three items, he told me to write them down. My explanation that I would go to my desk and write them was unsatisfactory.

"Get your pad and come back in here. I want you to make that to-do list right here."

"Yes, sir," I responded unquestioningly, even though I was a little puzzled by his making such a big deal out of this.

After I returned and prepared the short list, General Patton said, "Now, remember this. When you come through that door, you have a pocket notebook and a pen to write what I tell you. You make a list of everything and check it off with a completion note and the date.

"Things get very busy around here. You'll have good intentions of remembering my instructions, but when you go out that door, you'll be distracted by dozens of things. I don't want my instructions pushed aside by ringing phones, complaints, visitors, or anything else.

"There's one thing you need to understand. You won't get fired for any act of commission, but you'll lose your job in a minute for an act of omission. Failing to do something you should have done will get you fired. You got that?"

I responded with a definite, "Yes, sir," as I scribbled a note on my pad: "Don't forget nothing!"

General Patton knew that high stress suppresses short-term memory. I don't think General Patton cared about the effects of stress on my metabolism or my immune system, but he wanted a backup system for my short-term memory. Of course, I knew the importance of making notes during times of high stress. I'd even required my lieutenants to make notes during firefights. I just had not anticipated that working with General George Patton would bring a level of stress matched only by combat.

To overcome these same stressful situations in combat, leaders give simple, straightforward orders. Backup and redundant signals are planned to avoid tragic mistakes. For example, a commander and his radio operator make sure they both understand the circumstances for lifting friendly artillery fire as troops move into the target area. They remind each other and confirm when the orders are given.

Many business leaders have the same kind of arrangements with their administrative assistants, and both of them appreciate the reminders. Practicing these types of reminders during routine times ensures their effectiveness in times of crisis.

Sorting Them Out

Businesses and the Army are faced with the same mix of people—those who have developed a stress tolerance and those who are continually overwhelmed by something as simple as a misplaced order form. The process of sorting those who can handle stress from those who can't begins early in the military.

Remember those recruits who were met by the demanding drill sergeants? The Army's sorting process actually starts the night they arrive: training that physically and emotionally stretches the recruits toughens the capable ones. Drill sergeants have high expectations and demand perfection in the small things such as the proper wearing of uniforms, perfect organization of equipment, and attention to details when marching. The sergeants are loud and demanding, but they know when to encourage and mentor. Every day those young soldiers achieve at higher and higher levels.

Their positive reactions to stress help them achieve things they never thought possible. Physically unfit recruits are soon conditioned to run a mile, then five miles and more. Teenagers who never picked up their own bedrooms quickly become experts at cleaning, folding, and storing personal items. Surly, street-tough teens who never knew civil conversation quickly learn the benefits of saying "Yes, sir," and "No, sir." The discipline increases confidence. The repetitive stress situations help them see that they can perform in spite of threatening circumstances. Little by little, they gain a tolerance for stress.

Some people enter the military unprepared for even the smallest amount of stress, and they are overwhelmed by the circumstances of basic training. Their reaction to stress ranges from complete emotional breakdown to misbehavior that leads to their discharge from the Army. Drill sergeants and commanders are aware of this extreme possibility and prefer to guide each soldier to success, but the actions of some recruits make it impossible to guide them through the system.

With some modification, corporate leaders can use similar techniques to identify those who cannot tolerate any kind of stress and guide them to jobs where less is expected of them. To do this, some companies start every new employee in jobs that are menial but important to the success of the firm. People are tested and proven capable before being promoted to positions of responsibility. Other companies test the ability of new employees by making them assistants before giving them full responsibility. Few corporations have the luxury of shaping and molding employees the way the Army does, but it is possible to stress-test people by giving them increased responsibility, creating deadlines, and requiring higher and higher performance the more time they spend in their positions.

If people cannot meet expectations under stress, it makes little sense to promote them into high-stress positions. Both soldiers and corporate personnel need to function when things go wrong. Increasing stress tolerance needs to be done before the major crisis; otherwise, your people will collapse the way my mortar platoon leader did when he thought we were going to be overrun at the old French fort in Vietnam (see Chapter 1).

Here are some Army techniques you can use in your office to increase stress tolerance or to weed out those who cannot deal with stress:

• Establish deadlines that are just a little short of expectations. Shorten the time a couple of days to see how employees perform and to toughen their stress tolerance somewhat. Having employees hurry up and wait is better than having them scrambling at the last minute to meet deadlines.

• Change the requirements and demand maximum performance in spite of fluctuating circumstances. Employees are reassured when leaders demonstrate control, and less-tolerant employees control their stress to meet your expectations. The changes are frustrating, but people are emotionally tougher after responding to their leader's commanding presence.

• Demand perfect administrative and logistical support for yourself and others. Showing employees that total quality management is important during stressful periods illustrates that you are in control and that you have confidence in the planned outcome. Army leaders actually expect more of their support teams during a time of crisis and accept no excuses about short notice, inadequate provisions, or understaffing. They want results all the time, and this increases their team's tolerance to stress.

• Permit absolutely no backstabbing or criticism of fellow workers. Requiring employees to make only positive references toward others helps build trust, and it eliminates a major stressor when the pressure begins to grow. Army sergeants are not bashful as they order soldiers to stop criticizing others. The direct approach works best in this area because some employees are just prone to criticize someone or something all the time.

• Develop procedures, and expect everyone to comply. Everyone feels more in control when they follow established procedures. The Army is famous for operating by the book. Knowing that there is a prescribed procedure is comforting during a time of crisis. The more often soldiers see good results, the stronger they are in facing stress.

• Follow up on instructions to make sure the tasks are completed. This increases positive stress to get the job done as requested. It also increases tolerance to the follow-up that will come during times of crisis. The Army has a saying that the jobs you follow up on are the only jobs that get done. Everyone who has too much work takes the path of least resistance and assigns lower priority to those things that will not be followed up.

• Conduct strict inspections of records and performance. This is part of your high standards and expectations. Thorough audits identify problems and give you opportunities to compliment team members. Both your records and your people will be more prepared for stress-filled events. Every unit in the Army is subject to a major annual readiness inspection. Those who don't follow regulations in keeping records and completing training suffer the consequences at inspection time. Any amount of time they saved in short-cutting the system is lost as they work long hours getting ready for these major inspections. The shortcuts eventually increase stress.

• Require ongoing training and refresher courses—and test everyone's knowledge. One of the greatest stress controllers is being prepared. Well-trained people are also more tolerant of stress. Every unit in the Army has an annual training schedule for essential items. Part of the schedule is refresher training; part is training in new subjects. Some corporations maintain a similarly rigorous training schedule, but other companies see training as an expense instead of an investment. Less-trained employees are less tolerant of stress, and their skills fall behind the competitor who has an aggressive training program.

- Keep raising the bar of expectation in all areas. Accompanied by recognition for work well done, continually raising standards adds positive pressure and improves performance. Without the recognition, however, the higher standards contribute to a negative stress situation. As with the Army, ask more of your people during routine situations, and they will be better prepared in the face of obstacles.

Those who can handle stress continue to seek out challenges and are rewarded with greater responsibilities. Those who cannot handle increased stress are likely to be relegated to less stressful positions.

Listen to Your Own Advice

When stress runs high, people make mistakes and act illogically. Recent media stories exposed example after example of good people doing bad things. These people were just as smart as they ever were, but stress had dumbed down that special part of their brains that gave them control over their actions. Some of these people knew they shouldn't do certain illegal or immoral things, but stress weakened their inhibitions and made them incapable of changing their behavior.

> Don't be one of the great ones who are dragged down by stress.

It's one thing to prepare subordinate leaders for the stress they will confront, but you must also consider your own stress tolerance and whether you have what it takes to lead. If you fail to control your own stress, it will control you as you climb the corporate ladder— and on your way down. The opportunities for error are great when your mind is clouded by involuntary physical and emotional responses to stress.

If you recognize that your logical thinking is out of line, you should take action to control the stress instead of waiting for your name to show up in the media because of some temporary misjudgment. If you repeatedly do things that you know are improper, get some professional advice, or you risk wrecking your career and the lives of those around you.

Understanding how to control the benefits and hazards of stress gives you the edge in routine matters and times of crisis. Keep in mind the ways you can use positive stress to prepare people and help them achieve, but also remember that cumulative stress can undo your efforts. You need to strike a balance between the stress you create to get good results and the stress that diminishes performance.

Chapter 4 takes a look at how you can help your employees hold up in times of crisis and how the Army uses post-battle evaluations to see what went well or what needs more attention.

4

EXPOSING WEAKNESSES

★

American athletes grow up knowing that their coach will schedule a postgame review. Even if the team wins the game, they want to know what went right, what went wrong, and what they can do better next time. If their team lost, they want to know what changes need to be made so they can become winners. In practice, coaches use the same technique after running each play, helping everyone understand what went well and what needs more practice. Both the postgame and in-practice reviews control stress and build on positive reactions to increase confidence and improve performance.

The Army has its own version of postgame reviews. In the beginning, the Army used *after-action reports* to record events and collect historical data. This old type of report was sometimes called a "postmortem"—a dissection of what happened, who got the credit for successes, and who got the blame for what went wrong. These reports captured data, but they did nothing to improve performance or control stress. Commanders knew when more training was required and developed schedules for it, but there was little on-the-spot evaluation and improvement.

Today's "Reviews" Are Different from Yesterday's "Reports"

Today's after-action reviews are used the same way coaches use postgame and in-practice reviews. No longer is it simply a matter of recording a history of the event and fixing blame; today's reviews provide a dynamic, participatory communications process. To understand the difference between the two, consider the following interesting stories from the Army's history.

Students of the American Civil War still research after-action reports such as those written by Major General Franz Sigel, commanding officer of the Union's First Corps, Army of the Potomac, telling of his unit's participation in the Battle of Second Manassas. He reports on the First Corps' daylong efforts to defend a bridge against massing Confederate troops. Instead of protecting the bridge, however, his unit destroyed it when the enemy forded the river on either flank and threatened to surround the defenders.

In the midst of his withdrawal, General Sigel received orders changing his direction of march, sending him some distance away. In compliance with the directive, the tired soldiers marched the entire distance without resting. As the rear guard arrived at the destination, a horseman rode in with additional orders for him to attack across the original bridge at first light.

General Sigel writes of these conflicting orders in his very detailed after-action report, as he describes positioning of units, orders received, and overall results. He makes interesting comments on poor communications, but ultimately his document is only a report. It contains no information from subordinate commanders or frontline troops. Nor does it address what went right, what went wrong, and what could be done to improve future performance.

Reports like General Sigel's were the standard right up until World War II. The reports achieved their historical purpose, but they are nothing like the *after-action reviews* (AARs) used in today's Army.

In *SLAM: The Influence of S. L. A. Marshall on the United States Army*, author Deane Williams gives credit to the noted historian for making the transition from reports and debriefings to a structured AAR. Williams tells how Marshall traveled the front lines as an experienced journalist and Army historian, collecting firsthand accounts of what was going on. When Marshall arrived in the Pacific, he found that the island battles were unlike the mainland battles of Europe where actions continued uninterrupted for days and weeks. The island battles occurred during a defined period, allowing Marshall to interview troops en masse at the end of the action.

These interviews revealed valuable information about equipment, tactics, enemy capabilities, communications, and other such things for subsequent campaigns. Previously, unit leaders were aware of this kind of information on a piecemeal basis, but Marshall captured all of it in historical reports, which were then disseminated to other units so everyone could benefit.[1]

The traditional approach changed into a living, dynamic effort to learn from both successes and problems. Soldiers and their commanders commented on what they had observed, how well the objective was accomplished, what worked well, and which tactics needed to be changed. They talked about weapon problems, equipment that failed, and enemy tactics. Today, encouraging conversation about traumatic events is a primary method for controlling combat fatigue, and these group discussions went a long way in allowing soldiers to talk through the horrors of battle. Marshall's AARs were very different from the historical account written by General Sigel in the Civil War.

Following World War II, the Army adopted Marshall's strategy, collecting and disseminating battlefield tips and techniques in a process known as "lessons learned." As the Army passed through Korea, the Cold War, and Vietnam, a conscientious effort was made to collect this type of information, and a Center for Army Lessons Learned was established at Fort Leavenworth to print and distribute information that would help other units in similar situations.

In my own military training, the lessons learned played a key role in preparing soldiers for combat. For example, one of the lessons learned about booby traps remains to this day a vivid memory of my arrival in Vietnam. In the first couple of days, an experienced sergeant demonstrated several of the enemy's booby traps. Among them was a popular trap made of a small clay pot that had a heavy gauge flip-up wire fastener to secure the lid. The Vietcong used the clay pot as a lure because soldiers recognized it as a cheese container from the United States. It was shipped into Vietnam as a grocery store item, stolen by the enemy, or picked up after it was discarded by soldiers, and turned into a booby trap by connecting a grenade to it with a small piece of wire. Knowing some of the ways the Vietcong typically placed booby traps helped control stress as we moved about in enemy territory. Over the coming months, we found several such containers in villages and along paths, but the lessons learned from the AARs had taught us to leave them alone.

The Modern AAR

As is usual following major military conflicts, Army budgets were slashed after Vietnam. In addition, personnel cuts were implemented, and commanders throughout the Army sought to achieve more effective training with less funding. Both commanders and troops felt the stress of doing more with fewer troops and less money

It was in this period of budget restrictions that the Army's Training and Doctrine Command resurrected S. L. A. Marshall's review process for significant parts of training exercises as well as post-battle analysis, and this practice is now widely used. Commanders now improve their own operations and others by joining their troops to gather information before, during, and after training and at appropriate intervals on the battlefield. They schedule time for AARs and ask for soldier input on every aspect of the training and operation. Soldiers are encouraged to make their feelings and observations known. Commanders listen to the critical remarks to understand what is working for them, and they listen to suggestions for improving future actions.

A conscientious effort is made to uncover information that will help units perform better. No longer is the AAR a simple historical document where commanders record a singular perspective about battle operations. The AAR has become a management tool for improving operations and controlling stress through communications and soldier input. The opportunity to talk about what happened is an important factor in controlling stress, and the AARs give soldiers a chance to do just that. Soldiers who provide input feel more in control of their future and have greater confidence in leaders who value their observations.

Procedures for Doing AARs

One of the Army's field manuals, *Battle Focused Training* (FM 25-101), declares that AARs are a leadership responsibility and describes the reviews as professional discussions among leaders and participants to analyze "what was planned, what happened during the training, why it happened, and what could have been done differently to improve performance."[2] The same field manual recommends formally including AARs in lesson plans and operations orders, explaining that the AAR's purpose is to determine what can be done better next time, not whether the unit passed or failed the test.

The input of all participants is important in determining how events played out and what would improve performance. Because every member of the operation might have critical information for subsequent success, Army units incorporate as many possible players as space and continuing missions permit. Corporate employees can benefit from the same kind of AAR and control their stress in the same way as they talk about their observations and make recommendations.

The importance the Army places on AARs can be seen in the detailed planning as commanders:

- Prepare for AARs.
- Prepare and train observers to participate in training or operations.
- Conduct the AAR session itself.

To understand that detailed planning, let's examine each step.

Preparing for an AAR

Planning for an AAR is a critical part of the entire process. The Army field manual *Battle Focused Training* describes nine specific steps in preparing for the AAR. The steps are the same for training as for combat, and each of the steps has its own application in the execution of business training and operations.

1. **Establish objectives for the AAR.** The AAR is just as important as any other element in the training and operations process, so military and corporate leaders want to include AAR objectives, such as (a) achieve 100 percent participation at each AAR, (b) discuss the major elements of each action step, or (c) disseminate AAR information to all interested parties within 24 hours.

2. **Select qualified observers and provide additional training if necessary.** The observers must understand the training objectives and be experienced in the skills to be observed. They should be trained as observers, and they must not be assigned other duties during the exercise. Corporate use of observers can be focused on both the training and operational aspects of business. Business leaders can benefit greatly from the use of observers in the planning, implementation, and operation phases of projects and processes

3. **Review the plans for training and operations, as well as the evaluation.** Leaders need to make sure that these plans are up-to-date and that they include knowledge gained in previous AARs. A review of the AAR plan is important to make sure that it contains information important to leadership and that observers and participants know what will be evaluated.

4. **Identify the participants.** Commanders specify who will attend the AAR. If space permits, everyone not engaged in the continuing mission should participate, including observers and, in the case of the military, the commanders of the aggressor forces. Corporate AARs should be enjoyable events and include everyone associated with the project under discussion. If key individuals cannot attend, they should be interviewed for their input.

5. **Plan specific times for AARs during training exercises.** Leaders who plan for AARs maximize the learning experience and stress control if the AARs are completed after each segment of training. Successful corporate implementation of this process includes scheduling AARs prior to the kickoff of a project and after each significant event. Mid-phase AARs are also encouraged rather than allowing too much time to pass between meetings. Updates, progress reports, lessons learned, changes in direction, recommendations, and pleas for help are all topics for discussion. Leadership will benefit from the information exchange, and stress will be controlled as participants set the direction for future actions.

6. **Make potential site selections.** Selecting the AAR site prior to the training improves effectiveness and expedites the learning. While classrooms can be used, the training site itself is the preferred location for sharing information and for stress control. Businesses also prefer to conduct AARs on-site—for example, at the chemical lab, manufacturing plant, customer or vendor headquarters, transportation facility, warehouse, financial institution, academic building, and so on. AARs on home territory enhance stress control and individual participation.

7. **Select training aids.** Pre-positioning training aids, charts, and other graphic aids expedites the review and ensures that equipment is available when troops or employees arrive. Informal corporate AARs might have nothing more than a flip chart, but more sophisticated AARs might need the assistance of a meeting planner to make the event first-class. The meeting place should be ready when guests arrive and start on time. Sound systems with remote microphones permit audience input. Prepared PowerPoint presentations help keep the meeting focused, and impromptu slides made during the meeting help summarize remarks. The information exchange is the essential element of the AAR, far more important than the quality of the location.

8. **Prepare an AAR plan.** An outline of key points is essential to conducting the AAR. Leaders should include time for key players and observers to discuss objectives as they understood them, what took

place, key elements of the training, errors and problems encountered, and corrective actions required for better performance. Corporate AARs should use a similar agenda. Key participants should understand their role in the meeting and receive a draft agenda as soon as is practical, and everyone should have a copy a day or so prior to the AAR. The AAR facilitator should contact key participants well before the meeting to get an understanding of their initial contribution, their level of preparation, and their training aids requirements.

9. **Review the unit's training objectives and plans.** This step refreshes the leader's perspective on how this specific training fits into the overall plan. Corporate and military leaders should review all documents regarding the training or the project. If interim AARs have been conducted, leaders should review the summary of each AAR and include in the agenda any items requiring additional coverage.

Using this nine-step checklist helps leaders get the most out of AARs. The better the planning, the better the result, and the better the participation, the better the stress control. The second step of this process noted the importance of observers, and the following section provides details on their selection and participation.

Preparing and Training the Observers

The observers should be knowledgeable and respected people charged with monitoring performance and procedures during training or operations. Their only role during the event is to observe and report. Employees from various departments can be used as observers, if they can be objective in their reporting. Or outside consultants can be hired for specific training or operations. The Army simply assigns leaders from similar units to observe training exercises, and corporations could greatly benefit from consultation with industry experts who are familiar with similar operations.

The observer's reporting document can be as sophisticated as the leader chooses or as simple as a checklist with space for narrative observations. This report is given to the assembled group of participants at the AAR, but incorporating the observations into future operations is a leadership responsibility. The role of the observer is finished at the end of the final AAR.

The Army has established six specific steps for observers as they prepare for the AAR:

1. **Review the objectives, orders, and doctrine.** It is important for both the participants and the observers to understand the purpose and objectives of the training as well as the specific goals of projects and operations.

2. **Observe the training or business process.** A sufficient number of well-trained observers is essential to getting the most out of the AAR. The expense of trained observers may be substantial, but it should be included in the training or operations budget; their value in the process is worth the cost. Whether you're working with classroom training or hands-on processes, observers can help minimize the stress level of everyone involved and maximize your budget dollars and productivity.

3. **Organize the selected AAR site.** Observers might need additional personnel to organize the AAR site, because their full attention will be on the people involved in the training or operations. The observer team leader can coordinate with the AAR facilitator and meeting planners for special requirements.

4. **Collect information from other observers.** The observers are like baseball umpires in that each observer sees things from a unique perspective. Military or corporate leaders can designate which observer is responsible for specific phases or actions, or they can delegate this responsibility to the observer team leader. Either way, the observer team leader is responsible for collecting and organizing the information for the benefit of all participants.

5. **Develop a discussion outline.** Just as the AAR facilitator develops an agenda for the meeting, observer team leaders should develop an outline for their report. Outlines and summary notes can be provided to each participant.

6. **Organize and rehearse.** AARs are held immediately after each phase of the project or training. It isn't practical to conduct an AAR in the midst of battle, of course, but any pause in the fighting or the completion of a battle gives key participants a chance to evaluate how they are doing. Corporate leaders can schedule AARs at appropriate times.

Whenever it is practical, observers need to rehearse their role prior to the event. Similarly, corporate observers need to understand their roles and the reporting sequence. They also need to understand whether training aids or other essential tools will be available for their presentation.

Observers play a key role in stress control by providing an unbiased report on everything they have observed. Compliments on work well done can strengthen the confidence of participants. Open recognition of errors is equally encouraging, as people can understand what must be done to improve performance.

Conducting the AAR

The AAR meeting should be conducted by a facilitator rather than the highest-ranking team member. Commanders or corporate team leaders should be silent during the meeting unless they need to explain why they gave certain directives or to describe their other thought processes. Leaders can be brought into the conversation to find out, for example, why the decisions were made, additional information that would have been useful in making the correct decision, or what team members could have done to improve the decision-making process. As participants address leadership mistakes, they need to be respectful but open in their comments on the error.

The Army's field manual, *Battle Focused Training*, describes the important steps of the AAR process as follows:

1. **Restate the unit's mission or training objectives.** To get group participation immediately, facilitators often ask subordinate leaders

to restate the mission and training objectives to confirm that everyone correctly received and interpreted the organization's goals.

2. **Generate discussions.** This portion of the AAR is essential for evaluating the action. It also helps control stress by encouraging each participant to discuss his or her observations. The AAR facilitator's key task is to guide rather than to participate in the discussion. The AAR gets participants to discuss what happened and why, by using open-ended questions so participants respond with their own words instead of providing *expected* answers. Participants should be encouraged to include *why* things happened as well as *what* took place.

The following are sample questions:

- How well do you think we succeeded in accomplishing our mission?
- How well were the initial instructions and expectations communicated?
- How well suited was the equipment we used?
- What kind of instructions, equipment, or training would be helpful in future actions?

3. **Orient participants to training objectives.** Facilitators need to keep things on track and include each of the training objectives while preventing discussion of unrelated subtopics.

4. **Seek maximum participation.** The use of training aids and prompting questions should encourage input from all participants. Facilitators can draw nonparticipating individuals into the discussion by asking them questions that require explanations rather than yes-or-no answers. A level of comfort and trust will be established if you praise those who are participating and compliment them on the value of their observations.

5. **Emphasize key learning points by frequently summarizing what has been said.** AAR facilitators can enhance the review and encourage participation by relating the observations to the training

objectives. By repeating observations and meanings, facilitators can make sure they understand the issue, and the restatement might clarify the observations for others in the meeting.

Freedom of expression is very important if you want to expose weaknesses in your training or in the company. But if there is a perception of repercussions, no matter how remote or unintended, participants will not reveal weaknesses. The Army has discovered many shortcomings by encouraging honest and open AARs.

The Army's openness for the exposure of such weaknesses can be seen in "Avoid the Blues," by Ralph Nichols, an analyst for the Center for Army Lessons Learned. In the article, Nichols provides examples of shortcomings exposed in AARs for Operation Enduring Freedom (Afghanistan).[3] A few of the listed weaknesses are as follows:

- Improper identification of friendly and enemy troops that led to death by *friendly* fire
- Navigational errors that contributed to the deaths of American soldiers
- Inadequate fire control that resulted in Americans shooting artillery rounds at other Americans
- Ineffective control of units maneuvering in close proximity with other American units
- Casualties resulting from Americans accidentally entering *friendly* minefields
- Accidents resulting from weapons failures or poor troop discipline

If an organization as successful and as structured as the Army can be confident enough to log the preceding weaknesses, surely corporations can be brave enough to allow open discussion of weaknesses that are hampering progress in the marketplace. Companies that currently emphasize AARs find that people deal with stressful situations better when they participate in a review of their own performance and have some say in controlling their future.

Stress Control and AARs

In addition to using AARs to improve training and performance, Army leaders use them to control stress through improved communications and confidence building. Providing soldiers an opportunity to discuss in detail the training objectives and combat missions gives them confidence in their participation as well as a feeling that they have some say in their future, both of which are critical elements in stress control.

The AARs also provide an opportunity for unit leaders to observe how stress is affecting their troops. The early symptoms of battle fatigue can be seen in soldiers who complain bitterly about trivial matters and constantly criticize others. On the other hand, soldiers who make a positive contribution to AAR discussions, even if they do expose weaknesses, are probably less vulnerable to battle fatigue at that moment, and these soldiers can encourage and support those suffering from negative stress reactions.

The AARs are also opportunities for facilitators and unit leaders to praise individuals for outstanding performance and for contributing to the discussion. Such recognition contributes to increased confidence and unit cohesion. Just as most Army unit leaders do, corporate leaders can use AARs to increase performance while controlling stress in the workplace. Employees may not be shooting at each other or injuring themselves with malfunctioning weapons, but they are just as concerned with the quality performance of their company. They want to do a good job for the company, and they appreciate having a say in how things are being done.

Using AARs in the Corporate Setting

Following the Army's lead, some corporations have implemented formal AAR programs in their training, operations, and product development. Signet Consulting Group,[4] a company that facilitates corporate use of AARs, explains that AARs are key programs at corporations like BP Amoco, Motorola, General Electric, Steelcase, and Harley Davidson. BP Amoco, they say, has followed the Army's lead in building the AAR process into project management. Before, during, and after analysis of each major step, the following questions are asked:

- What was supposed to happen?
- What actually happened?
- Why was there a difference?
- What can we learn from this?

In 1999, *Fortune* magazine writer Thomas A. Stewart discussed BP Amoco's use of AARs and explained how this strategy saved them more than $80 million in a single project.[5] Amoco's AAR process solicited information from every oil industry colleague with knowledge of opening new oil fields and ideas on how to cut costs. They were criticized for spending so much research time instead of drilling holes, but in the end, they found a profitable way to drill for oil in a North Sea field previously considered impossible. The $80 million is just what they saved in drilling expenses and does not address the huge profits Amoco will enjoy because they conquered this "impossibility."

AARs are also a topic of discussion in the area of knowledge management as more and more companies see results from using this method of sharing information and avoiding mistakes. Knowledge management expert Daryl Morey reports that Texas Instruments saved $1.5 billion by gathering information from their various fabricating plants on how to increase productivity and avoid building two new plants.[6] Knowledge management expert, Verna Allee, reports that Chevron also saved $1.4 billion between 1992 and 1997 through their best-practices initiatives and information sharing programs.[7]

Now test the process yourself by engaging in a simple impromptu AAR focused on routine actions. If you also want to get a feel for how the process affects stress levels, you can take an informal poll prior to your AAR. Compare the results with another survey done after everyone has a chance to participate with their thoughts, ideas, and observations about what was supposed to happen, what actually happened, why there was a difference, and what can be learned from the effort.

People enjoy solving problems and making their team stronger; they like being in control of their future. If you ask them for their opinions and observations, you'll be surprised by the quality and depth of their response. The next chapter continues the discussion of the importance of information and communications.

Notes

1. Deane Williams, *SLAM: The Influence of S. L. A. Marshall on the United States Army*. Printed by the U.S. Army in 1990 and reprinted by the U.S. Army Center for Military History in 1994.
2. Army field manual FM 25-101, *Battle Focused Training*, Appendix G, "After Action Reviews," Headquarters, Department of the Army, Washington, D.C., September 30, 1990.
3. "Avoid the Blues," Ralph D. Nichols, JRTC CALL Analyst, Fort Leavenworth, KS, and After-Action Report of the 2-7 Mechanized Infantry (MECH IN) Battalion (BN), 3rd Infantry Division, Operation Iraqi Freedom.
4. Marilyn J. Darling and Charles S. Parry, *From Post Mortem to Living Practice: An In-depth Study of the Evolution of the After Action Review*, The Signet Consulting Group, Boston, MA, 2000.
5. Thomas A. Stewart, "Telling Tales at BP Amoco," *Fortune*, June 7, 1999.
6. Daryl Morey, "High-Speed Knowledge Management: Integrating Operations Theory and Knowledge Management for Rapid Results," e-article from *Journal of Knowledge Management*, Vol. 5, No. 4. 2001: MCB University Press.
7. Verna Allee, "Chevron Maps Key Processes and Transfers Best Practices," Knowledge, Inc., April 1997.

5

INFORMATION AND COMMUNICATIONS

★

Complex Army Communications

An extremely complex communications system is essential in running an organization as large as the U.S. Army. Commanders at the highest levels receive and distribute information around the globe. Radio and hard-wired networks provide unique as well as redundant communications support, operating at all of the known transmission frequency ranges. The system involves communication throughout the Army command as well as interservice networking with the Air Force, Marines, Navy, Coast Guard, and numerous governmental agencies, including those of the United States, host nations, and allies.

To make this work, the Army organizational structure includes signal units in support of all major commands, from battalion level right up to the Oval Office. Signal units manage communications from the White House and Air Force One with the same concern they give the radio communications of frontline soldiers. They don't carry the radios for those GIs, but they do help maintain them and configure communication procedures. The equipment for these signal units includes a variety of handheld and vehicle-mounted radios, such as walkie-talkies, durable combat radios, and cell phones, as well as sophisticated long-range communications equipment rivaling space-age technology. And every piece has been through strenuous testing that would challenge the most exhaustive comparisons by *Consumers Digest*.

Technology Can Help, but Face-to-Face Is Better

While communications strategies must constantly evolve to keep up with technological advancements and weapons systems, the people operating the systems remain pretty much the same as they have been throughout history. Modern soldiers are formally educated, computer savvy, and better equipped, but they need the same kind of tender-loving-care leadership as anyone else to overcome battlefield stress and win the fight.

As shown in previous chapters, soldiers—and employees—handle stress better under the following conditions:

- There is strong unit identity, esprit de corps, and high morale.
- They are given a good understanding of the mission and individual roles.
- Leadership cares about them as individuals.
- Accurate information takes the place of rumors.
- They believe in the cause they are working for.
- They all have confidence in their equipment and training and the support of supervisors.

Just as would be expected, studies done after Just Cause (Panama, 1989) and Desert Shield/Storm (Persian Gulf, 1990–91) showed that "battlefield leadership at all levels is an element of combat power."[1] And an essential element of that battlefield leadership is communication. Whether in combat or corporate business, communication is the element that guarantees all other leadership skills. If leaders cannot communicate with their team, either technologically or through interpersonal skills, their leadership is ineffective.

When there is a crisis—when confronting the enemy—the best communication between leaders and followers is face-to-face. Leaders need to be with combat units to understand the full scope of what is taking place in their sector, to guide tactical maneuvers, to encourage individuals, and to motivate their unit.

The same thing goes for communication between corporate leaders and employees. The leaders need to be present. They need to understand what their employees face. They need to be involved enough to encourage, motivate, and build esprit. Leaders who communicate well in person motivate both soldiers and employees. In my own sales management experience, I found that my time with salespeople was crucial to my understanding of the situation. In our informal, one-on-one conversations, we were always able to develop ideas and explore options. The individual salespeople easily informed me of customer needs, and I found that I could provide access to information and alternatives they couldn't obtain without my presence. Memos and phone calls are poor substitutes for personal communication.

Commanders must have interpersonal communication skills as well as technical skills. They need to know how to coordinate their efforts with other units, communicate with higher and lower commands, and use their battlefield equipment. However, their entire set of technical skills is diminished if they lack personal communication skills to motivate their soldiers.

Combat Communications Strategies

Memos and letters serve well to communicate technical information or to record commendations, but a personal conversation goes much further in gathering information from employees and communicating the meaning behind your words. As you improve communications within your company, you will find people less stressed over routine situations and more optimistic about their own performance. The change of attitude will have an impact on your bottom line.

Consider the importance of communications among soldiers going into battle. These soldiers run the risk of being maimed or killed at any minute, yet the commanders get them to perform. Some people may quickly conclude that these troops are under orders, so the leader just tells them to take their guns and move forward . . . against bigger guns, tanks, cannons, airplanes, bombs, napalm, chemical agents, and who knows what else.

Well, it just doesn't work that way. People need more than just an order to go into a stressful situation where they could be killed. They need to be motivated. They need leadership. They need to be a part of a team whose bond is so strong that a soldier will lay down his life for another. Their loyalty to the cause of defending American interests and other people has to be so strong that they are willing to suffer hardships and the threats of combat without questioning their own safety.

If Army commanders can get soldiers to take this kind of risk, corporate leaders can get employees to show up on time, put in a full day, make those cold calls, run the machines properly, put in orders on time, finish their work, practice their selling skills, negotiate the best deals, send out invoices, collect receivables, enter data, write programs, and so on. If soldiers can be motivated to face bullet-shooting, bayonet-carrying, hate-in-their-eyes enemies, business employees should be willing to do whatever it takes to keep the company going, keep their jobs, and keep food on their tables. If leaders can't motivate their troops to face the enemy, they will lose the battle.

Leadership communication is essential in motivating people and reducing stress. In a presentation to the Industrial Accident Prevention Association, the CEO of the Global Business and Economic Roundtable on Addiction and Mental Health, Bill Wilkerson, spoke of the top ten sources of modern-day workplace stress. In the following list, the number one ranking is the most stressful, but all ten of them have to do with leadership communications. Here is the countdown with Wilkerson's terms in quotation marks.

10. "The treadmill syndrome" causes employees to have too much or too little to do, have too many responsibilities, and work around the clock—even when away from the workplace.

9. "Random interruptions," such as telephone calls, walk-in visits, and sudden demands from a supervisor, keep employees from getting their work done.

8. "Pervasive uncertainty" created by constant, unsatisfactorily explained, or unannounced change causes stress.
7. "Mistrust, unfairness, and vicious office politics" keep everyone on edge and uncertain about the future.
6. "Unclear policies and no sense of direction in the company" cause additional uncertainty and undermine confidence in management.
5. "Career and job ambiguity" creates a feeling of helplessness and lack of control. (How can I succeed if I don't know what's expected of me or if my job here is uncertain?)
4. "No feedback, good or bad," prevents people from knowing how they are doing and whether or not they are meeting expectations.
3. "No appreciation" for employee participation generates stress that endangers future efforts.
2. "Lack of communications" up and down the chain of command leads to decreased performance and increased stress.
1. "Lack of control" is the greatest stressor in the workplace because employees become highly stressed when they feel they have no control over their participation or the outcome of their work.

Wilkerson sees each of these stressors as having an effect on mental health in the workplace. He concludes that business leaders can—and should—do something about each of them. He states that both men and women are de-motivated when their leaders fail to take action on these items.

Leaders who see their employees as the problem will continue having problems. People need leaders who are willing to do their own jobs in support of the work they require of team members. Leaders must communicate well to alleviate these ten problems if they want to control stress and help others do their best. In line with the previous observations about the effects of stress, the leaders who fail to communicate clearly and directly are the ones who contribute to stress levels within the company and compound the other problems.

Wilkerson continues by saying that money isn't what motivates people; instead, what motivates people are a balanced workload; control in the workplace; clear communications that remove fear, doubt, and mistrust; information that tells them where the company is going and their individual role; fair performance management; and an occasional note of appreciation.

Steps to Reduce the Top Ten Communication Stressors

So just how does an effective leader reduce these top ten stressors? Through good communications, of course, as leaders work with employees to preclude stressful situations or to help resolve the issues causing negative stress reactions.

Treadmill Syndrome: Too Much or Too Little to Do

A certain amount of work overload creates positive stress that leads to higher productivity as employees try harder and get more done, but an impossible workload creates negative stress reactions that reduce productivity. When there is clearly too much work to do and management obviously is unconcerned about employee welfare, employees simply slow down to survive the stress they feel.

To preclude this type of problem in the Army, leaders assign tasks, monitor workloads, and set priorities for subordinates. As discussed in Chapter 3, "soldiers only do what gets inspected," and leaders who shortcut the job-monitoring process soon discover that lack of supervision leads to shoddy work.

Communications in the corporate workplace are just as important. Those who overload employees and fail to communicate well wind up with highly stressed employees and lowered productivity. I once knew a sewing room manager who supervised more than fifty employees, and they all worked like mad to meet production. They seldom produced the required pieces per day, and there was little opportunity for interpersonal communications. Morale was terrible, complaints were many, and absenteeism was rampant. People didn't understand the purpose of their work. No one felt appreciated, and everyone distrusted management.

The single manager was as distraught as the employees because she had more responsibilities than one person could do: ordering supplies, making shipments, completing administrative tasks, directing maintenance, and handling all individual complaints. The supervisor was at her office at least three hours beyond quitting time, and she took work home with her every day to meet quotas. The stress affected her own productivity and her health.

The sewing room experienced high personnel turnover among the employees and supervisors. Having fewer supervisors may seem to have saved the company some money, but in actuality, the company probably spent more than they saved on hiring and training all the new employees while their production suffered. What the company really needed was to increase staff and thereby improve communications, reduce stress, and increase productivity.

Random Interruptions

Both managers and employees are frustrated by the numerous interruptions that interfere with their work. Except for the occasional personal visits, the interruptions are usually more important to the person calling or dropping by your desk. Everyone would be less stressed if they could find a way to control these interruptions, but the solution is held by management, not by those who constantly interfere with the work to be done.

We need to address two distinct categories of interruptions here— (1) management interruptions that prevent employees from doing their work, and (2) interruptions that keep managers from taking care of business.

First, those managers who constantly interrupt employees with miscellaneous demands must realize that their impromptu actions are counterproductive. Bosses who constantly demand immediate response for customer information, production data, file folders, and printouts might feel authoritative, but they are, instead, illustrating their own lack of organization and keeping employees from doing important work.

These inconsiderate leaders expect employees to drop whatever they are doing, break off phone conversations, leave meetings, or come all the way across the office to provide the information requested. Unlike well-organized managers, these *stress-making* supervisors fail to understand the importance of setting up information systems that permit logical presentation of the information on a periodic basis and storage of critical data within arm's length. Instead of completing work they are paid to do, these interrupted employees are acting as data clerks and finding themselves stressed because of the conflicting demands.

Second, many managers feel this same kind of stress. Both the tyrants and the well organized often find themselves torn between doing the *important* and taking care of the *urgent*. Just as managers can control the stress they cause employees, they can also control the stress they feel from constant interruptions.

When leaders and managers fail to delegate authority along with responsibility, employees seek approval or guidance for every decision and action, and the number of interruptions increases. When leaders communicate their intentions and employees have the authority needed to do their jobs, stress is reduced and employees no longer have to walk that fine line between what is allowed and what someone else must decide.

If you are the sole source for information, consider recording the information or establishing alternative sources to enable employees to work on their own. Logbooks, policy manuals, and information networks can reduce employee dependence on management and each other.

New Army leaders learn skills for controlling interruptions while getting the job done and reducing stress. Specifically, officers and sergeants are taught to do the following:

- Maintain frequent face-to-face communications with soldiers
- Delegate authority as well as responsibility

- Communicate goals and principles so others know how the leaders would respond
- Structure the times that the leaders are available to field questions

These same techniques can work for you and all of your employees. Each step requires some discipline and direct communications about your efforts to reduce interruptions. Most people, however, will readily adopt your plan and make an effort to be more self-reliant.

No Appreciation

Of course, you appreciate your employees. You can't do all of the work yourself, so you need these people to get things done. You pay them well, and they have all of those hotshot fringe benefits—health insurance, retirement plans, holiday pay, and maybe even a turkey at Thanksgiving. They're on the payroll, and their checks are larger than those from most businesses in the community. You have a perfect company safety record. You even provide free coffee and soft drinks in the break room. So why do so many employees feel unappreciated? Poor communications—that's why.

Even though companies spend thousands of dollars a year on employees, they don't see it as a form of appreciation. You can list all of your employees' benefits and show how these perks actually double employee compensation. But rather than appreciate that fact, some employees will see your document as a way of bragging about yourself.

People feel appreciated when someone takes the time to listen to them, ask about their families, and understand what they are going through at home, at school, or at work. They also feel valued when leaders compliment them on a job well done, even if their accomplishment is simply always being on time.

If you want to find out what makes people feel appreciated, go to a retirement dinner or a going-away party and listen to the remarks people make. If the departing person is a dud, the remarks are going to reflect that person's incompetence in a joking but revealing way.

However, if people admire the honored guest, you'll find out that it doesn't take much to make people feel appreciated. Remarks like the following tell you what is important:

- "I remember when she came to my daughter's funeral. That's when I knew how important I was to the company."
- "All of you remember when we had that shutdown. Wasn't it great how he let us know what was going to happen ahead of time? If we hadn't heard about the changes, I'd have been stuck with a new mortgage that I couldn't afford."
- "I don't know how he did it, but I saw him on the shop floor everyday. He always came by and greeted me and asked about my family."
- "You know, the thing I appreciate most are the company picnics she started. She always served the potato salad herself, and she cleaned up when it was over. She's just one of us."

All of these examples and most of what you'll hear at the going-away celebration will be about personal communications. There might be some mention of a leader's commendable acquisition posture or their financial responsibility, but the business achievements are usually left in the boardroom. What motivates and inspires people is the personal communication.

The same situation exists in the Army. Leadership changes frequently, but those leaders who clearly appreciate their subordinates are far more respected than tyrants who issue orders and administer punishment. Those who communicate their appreciation for soldiers' efforts might even expect more out of their troops than do tyrants, but GIs suffer much less from negative stress reactions and are ready and willing to give their all when they know their work is appreciated. Just like their civilian counterparts, military leaders are remembered for their ability to communicate their appreciation.

Leaders challenged with managing large numbers of people or with remote operations can personalize their communications by putting a touch of themselves on the high-tech tools. Sterile announcements can be personalized by merging first names into documents along with short, personal notes. Everyone appreciates your attention to their welfare and your interest in their families.

Personal follow-up telephone calls mean a lot to those involved in conference calls, bridge lines, or e-mails. You can make notes about individual input during the electronic meeting and follow up by phone to show employees that you were listening and you care about their ideas or comments. Your calls to explore subjects in detail can motivate people for future input and develop some profitable ideas.

Simple, personalized remarks written on the face of routine memos can make all the difference to employees who otherwise do their jobs and clock out at quitting time. Your attaboy remarks might be the only compliments some people ever receive. Some of these meaningful remarks will become "souvenirs" that are kept forever.

I recently received a phone call from an officer I knew in the Army more than thirty years ago. I was impressed that he remembered me and took the time to track me down. When I asked what made this possible, he told me that he still had a memo he had prepared for me. He kept the document because I had penned a compliment in the margin, thanking him for his efforts.

If you do make notes of your appreciation, include the employee's first name with your compliment, and you'll be surprised at what this short communication does for morale and productivity. If you can make comments on items going home with people, you can affect the morale of the entire family. If your staff size permits, you can write a personal note right on their paycheck, such as "Thanks, Bob. We couldn't have shipped that big order without your help this week."

Some people will stop you to thank you for the note. Some will even write you a thank-you note. Sincere notes to your people pay big dividends.

> The greatest compliment that was ever paid me was when one asked me what I thought, and attended to the answer.
>
> **—Henry David Thoreau**

Army units typically recognize superior achievement with medals and honors, and daily involvement is highlighted with framed certificates of appreciation, letters of com-

Key Phrases for Complimenting People on Their Work

Well done.

Good work.

Keep up the good work.

This is excellent.

Nice timing.

Good advice.

Insightful.

Good perception.

One of the best ideas I've heard this year.

Good teamwork.

Awesome.

Brilliant.

You hit a home run.

Go for it.

Let's talk about this great idea.

Thanks.

Thanks again.

mendation, public announcement of achievements, three-day passes (extra vacation), and documents recognizing the families' volunteer efforts. Awards ceremonies are emphasized, and commanders make an effort to include family members so they can see how much their GI is appreciated.

Every manager can afford the time to be courteous, attentive, and caring. If you don't have enough hours in the day to exchange remarks with employees, maybe you need to look at the stressors in your own life and reorganize or delegate certain tasks to recover the time it takes to be involved with your employees on a personal level.

Showing your concern for ongoing work is appreciated just as much as formal recognition for special accomplishments. You can make employees feel special and get a lot of information by asking, "How's it going with the X project that you wanted to have done next week?" or "Is there anything I can do to help you get Y done on schedule?" The added communication will more than pay for itself in improved productivity and increased profits.

Using One Technique to Control Seven Stressors

As mentioned earlier, clear communications can help control all of the top ten corporate stressors. Three stressors have already been discussed in detail: treadmill syndrome, random interruptions, and no appreciation. Now you'll discover how well-conducted meetings can help you control the remaining seven stressors:

- Pervasive uncertainty
- Mistrust, unfairness, and vicious office politics
- Unclear policies and no sense of direction in the company
- Career and job ambiguity
- No feedback
- Lack of communications
- Lack of control

Many people have attended so many poorly conducted meetings that they shudder just to think of putting a meeting reminder on the calendar. Over the years, I, too, became so disenchanted with the regularly scheduled weekly or monthly meetings that I simply discontinued them, and that was a big mistake.

I didn't like wasting everyone's time in meetings where individuals reported on activities about which no one else was concerned. I could easily see the ambivalence among those who were not reporting at the moment. My employees were so bored with the meetings that they immediately liked the idea of switching to one-on-one meetings with me. Subsequently, however, these same employees changed their minds and wanted to return to the group format.

While the one-on-one meetings updated me on their projects, which is what the earlier group meetings accomplished, everyone missed the exchange of technical information and the opportunity to socialize with others who worked in the same arena. During the period of one-on-one meetings, we also found an increase in uncertainty about how employees were doing as individuals and where the company was going. Some felt a degree of uncertainty about their own jobs, and others complained about a lack of communications and feedback. The most popular complaint mirrored Wilkerson's number one reason for workplace stress: employees felt like they had *lost control* of their internal company contacts and information networks. In other words, the group meetings I had discounted were contributing much more than just the exchange of information. Instead of discontinuing the meetings, we should have worked harder to make the meetings more productive.

When we resumed the group meetings, we used effective meeting procedures such as those recommended in the Army field manual FM 22-101, *Leadership Counseling*. Instead of the reports my employees had been providing, we worked on creating opportunities and solving problems, one of the first recommendations in the Army's guidelines. First, we defined the opportunity or problem. Then we gathered the facts and decided upon alternatives. Everyone helped weigh the alternatives and made recommendations on the best approach. A preliminary plan was developed before the meeting was over, and those responsible could go to work on it as soon as the meeting concluded.

At subsequent meetings, everyone wanted an update on the success of the plans to which they had contributed. Meeting participants were attuned to the agenda items and anxious to put their knowledge to work. The standard reporting information was submitted by memo or discussed in separate one-on-one meetings. All seven of the stressors in the preceding bulleted list were affected by the valuable communications that resulted from changing the meeting strategies.

Since then, I've used all of the high-tech meeting tools such as e-mail, chat rooms, e-bulletin boards, blog sites, conference calls, bridge lines, videoconferencing, teleseminars, and webinars, but none of these is as valuable as the personal feel of a face-to-face meeting when it comes to good communications and stress control. The high-tech tools are still valuable, but people need to remember that there is much more to a meeting than just the reporting of information.

Pervasive Uncertainty Erodes Confidence

Employees prefer to hear accurate information about changes directly from management, rather than hear rumors of change from peers. Give them the facts and help them understand what the change means to the company and to them personally. Frequent meetings and communication can quickly clear up rumors.

In addition to the regular meetings, memos, letters of explanation, announcements, and personal updates are critical during times of uncertainty. Even if your company is not involved, you need to take action fast to head off employee concerns when the evening news carries stories about other companies and their trouble with plant closings, layoffs, or other problems. Assure your employees that your company has things under control, or admit that you have similar problems. The truth will minimize stress and open communication channels so everyone can be part of the solution.

Rumors prevail in the corporate workplace and in the Army. Good leadership and clear communication can put to rest the uncertainty that comes with frequent changes and fast-paced operations.

Office Politics and Mistrust Put People on Edge

Strong leadership in meetings can go a long way in exposing office politics and mistrust. A public demonstration of your disapproval of blatant office politics can build trust and rein in those who would take advantage of others. The meetings give people a chance to take credit for their own accomplishments.

Encourage all supervisors to give credit to subordinates. Demonstrate this by your own actions. Reward those who credit subordinates instead of taking credit themselves. Discipline those who fail to give credit where it is due.

Address rumors and half-truths wherever you find them. On-the-spot corrections are important, and encouraging open communications will alleviate mistrust. If you unintentionally mislead employees, admit your errors and make up for it in some way.

Many leaders feel that their authority is diminished if they admit mistakes, but I've learned that just the opposite is true in both the military and the corporate workplace. Openly admitting errors in judgment and appropriate rectification of the damage done can strengthen employee respect for leaders.

Career and Job Ambiguity Lead to Personnel Turnover

Career and job ambiguity might come from a vague understanding of responsibilities, but this is easily controlled with adequate job descriptions and personal coaching. Greater ambiguity occurs, however, from uncertainty about the company's future. Flat management structure and functional reporting can add to the uncertainty and confusion if leaders cannot meet with employees frequently.

Strong leaders who do communicate with employees will know whether the ambiguity is a problem that needs personal development or whether the problem can be solved by providing some reassurance about what lies ahead. Open discussion of these subjects in your meetings can help alleviate the problem and reduce your employee turnover.

Just as with pervasive uncertainty, good leaders address the wide range of issues that generate job ambiguity. You can recognize national situations that cause job ambiguity by watching the news or reading *USA Today* and the *Wall Street Journal*. If economic conditions, plant closings, and industry fluctuations make headline news, you can bet these articles will be of interest to your employees.

You might want to designate a trusted, high-ranking employee to be your eyes and ears on community matters that can create stress among employees. This same person can also advise you on how to de-stress the situation for employees, e.g., meetings, explanations, or actions.

Keep People Informed to Control Stress

The remaining four stressors on Wilkerson's list are related issues that, too, can be corrected through well-structured routine meetings. Employees who complain about having no control over their situations will also feel there is inadequate feedback, no appreciation, and poor communications.

Functional meetings can communicate both feedback and appreciation as you encourage participants to help set the course and solve the problems. Leaders who engage employees on this level find less stress, less turnover, and increased productivity. It isn't important that the CEO schedule these meetings, because the meetings are more productive if held at the team or department level where everyone can participate and the issues are relevant to everyone attending the meeting.

The traditional morning formations used by Army units serve well to assemble the troops for the day's work, but their purpose is dissemination of information from the top down. The real exchange of information and valuable communication occurs in the smaller group meetings when the platoon leaders and squad leaders work with their smaller teams.

One Army general I know used to have one lunch a week with junior officers who would otherwise never have an extended conversation with a general officer. The general used these meetings to get a pulse of what was going on in the ranks, so to speak, and to listen to the concerns of these junior officers. He answered questions, talked about the future, and explained policies and procedures that affected these officers and their soldiers. The general had a staff member take notes and provide feedback on any question that could not be answered on the spot. When the meetings were over, those attending felt like they were on the inside track, and everyone appreciated the follow-up communication on their subject of concern.

You don't have to be a CEO to use this general's communication strategy. No matter what your rank, you can invite team members to have lunch with you once a week. If you eat at the office, bring enough for you and the people attending the meeting. Your small investment in buying lunch will go a long way in successful communications and stress control.

Chapter 6 builds upon the importance of communications and discusses the necessity of being prepared on the battlefield and in the workplace.

Notes

1. Susan Canedy, ed., U.S. Army Training and Doctrine Command (TRADOC) Pamphlet 525-100-1, *Leadership and Command on the Battlefield. Operation Just Cause and Desert Storm* (Fort Monroe, VA: TRADOC, 1992), cover, 13, 17, and 41.

6

BEING PREPARED

★

You have little time to prepare when a crisis is upon you. Frequently, you just have to struggle through tough times as best you can and focus on being better prepared next time. Say you miss getting a big sale because of your poor sales presentation. Certainly you can brush up on your skills before the next opportunity, but that sale is gone forever. Or say you cannot accept an order because of inadequate manufacturing capacity. You definitely can get additional equipment before customers place the next big order, but you'll never replace the revenue lost on the one you missed. Likewise, if you have been caught by out-of-control stress that damaged your business and the productivity and health of your employees, you are losing money that you cannot replace. Well-prepared companies don't get caught unprepared; they are always ready for the present and for extraordinary events that typically derail those who do not prepare ahead of time.

Leaders are responsible for preparing themselves and their employees for whatever might occur. In the previous examples, well-prepared companies could have avoided the crises caused by inadequate presentation skills, poor manufacturing forecasts, and inadequate stress control. In other words, sound preparation helps leaders improve productivity and avoid some of the stress that would otherwise distract them even further.

As Army leaders prepare for the future, they know that they are personally responsible for preparing their soldiers for combat and making sure they are ready for battle. Regulations and standing orders dictate training, testing, and frequent refresher courses for individuals and units. Well-trained soldiers have been tested, and they know that they can perform in the face of great danger. They are confident in their ability to control stress and meet the enemy.

An infinite number of details require attention as leaders prepare to meet the enemy. Each type of military unit has unique requirements as they get ready for combat, but the three common areas of focus are as follows:

1. Education
2. Practice
3. Confidence in self and in equipment

Actually, most companies consider their employees and managers to be well prepared. But through my consulting work I've discovered that it takes only a little probing to see that additional corporate training is needed in three areas previously mentioned. The added confidence and operational ability that come with being prepared will improve performance and profitability and help control stress in the entire company.

Education and Training Are Fundamental in Controlling Stress

In just a few short weeks of training, the Army teaches every soldier the basics of Army life, such as marching, saluting, and marksmanship. Immediately after the basic training, enlisted soldiers move into specific courses of study for their military occupational specialty, and officers proceed to the basic officer courses. Each level of training prepares these people for unique jobs, and the better trained they are, the less stress they encounter at the next level.

Upon graduation from these second-level courses of instruction, soldiers are assigned to units where organizational-level instruction continues to prepare them for specific work in that outfit and laying the groundwork for a career-long education process. The Army structures education to prepare soldiers for both current and future assignments. The education doesn't stop, regardless of the years of service or the level of rank. Experience has shown that all of this education pays off in increased capability, confidence, and sense of control, all of which are essential ingredients in controlling stress.

Some of the best corporations also have well-structured, career-long programs to educate and train employees. Additionally, many of these companies have educational assistance programs to help employees earn undergraduate and graduate degrees. Some companies, however, do not have these programs and give no attention at all to educating employees beyond job-essential skills.

No matter what financial support is available in your company, your own education should be a priority. Take advantage of all the assistance your company provides, and pay for it yourself if there is no continuing education program in your company. Just like those military leaders, you need to know all you can about your company, competitors, customers, technology, and other classic corporate issues.

Excellent military leaders keep up with new equipment and techniques introduced into the Army, but they are also historians and explorers. They stay in touch with academia to include the latest scholarly research in their field and subscribe to business journals to understand the latest in corporate America. New and innovative approaches become apparent to those who read their industry's journals and business-related periodicals, such as *Wall Street Journal*, *Business Week*, and *Fast Company*. If you want to really excel, subscribe to the journals related to your industry to find out what's hot and what's working.

Many of the things you should know are free of charge if you research the library, the World Wide Web, and your company. The information is available in the public domain. Quiz yourself by looking at the items listed in the sidebar on the next page, and see how prepared you really are.

Some Army officers I know have taken it upon themselves to learn much more than the Army requires. They have completed every authorized level of training and almost every correspondence course offered by the various Army schools. Their goal is to be as knowl-

Nine Things to Know About Business Classics

1. **Leaders you admire:** How can you be like them?
2. **Legendary successes:** What did they do to reach the top?
3. **Companies who have beat all the odds** (and those who have failed): How did they do it?
4. **Case studies:** How often do you review case studies for various economic conditions and successes?
5. **Training literature:** Have you used training literature to refresh skills for yourself and others?
6. **Innovative journals:** Do you review cutting-edge journals to see what the fringe is thinking about?
7. **Journals from your customers' industries:** How else can you know what they need?
8. **Journals from your own industry:** How do you know what's going on if you don't spend time in your own journals?
9. **Classic business literature:** Do you have a good understanding of people and cultures?

edgeable as possible about what is going on in every branch of service and in other armies of the world.

The value of this type of education should be understandable to all corporate leaders. For example, how much do your key people know about your competitors? The competition should not be a subject only for your salespeople, because the more each department understands about their competing counterpart, the more competitive your company will become. Customer service managers should know the service strategies of each competitor. Accounting department managers should know the exact procedures used by competitors for billing, collections, credit approval, and financing. Distribution managers should know as much about the competition as they know about their own procedures, documentation, inventory levels, freight rates, and negotiating tactics. If your finance and accounting managers understand the procedures, processes, and equipment used by each of your competitors, they can help you structure your own departments to contribute to the company's competitive posture.

If your people don't know the competition in detail, they probably respond in crisis mode when competitors try to take your business. Their stress will be much lower if they are the ones who know the most about what is going on in the market.

Practice Is the Second Step in Being Prepared

Learning a subject is just the first step in being prepared. If you're not ready to apply the knowledge when the time comes, you won't be any better off than if you never learned it in the first place.

Everyone has grown up with the parental admonishment of "Practice until you get it right," or "Practice makes perfect." Army education echoes the same theme, as they require everyone, even the

---

Seven Things to Know About Your Company's Products

1. **The products you are involved with:** Where do they come from and how are they used?
2. **All of your company's products:** Do you know about *all* the products and not just the ones you're responsible for?
3. **Manufacturing operations and concerns:** Do you understand the needs and concerns of your other departments?
4. **Product development:** How well do you know your own people, projects, customer needs, and suppliers?
5. **Scheduling:** What are your company's strategies, concerns, and improvement projects?
6. **Shipping and distribution:** How does this affect production, sales, and opportunities?
7. **Service strategies:** What do your customers need, and what's going on in the various industries?

Five Things to Know About Your Company's Administrative Support

1. **Administrative procedures:** How do they affect people throughout the company?
2. **Accounting department:** What are their goals, concerns, and profit improvement strategies?
3. **Computer gurus:** Are you working with these people to improve productivity and increase profits?
4. **Employees:** Do you know their names, backgrounds, families, concerns, and ambitions?
5. **Management:** Do you know their experience, vision for company, and families?

experts, to keep practicing their skills. Most combat units have annual training cycles that repeat previously learned skills, including annual tests to help everyone understand the skills they have maintained as well as those that need more work.

Just as soldiers practice their technical skills and marksmanship, your corporate employees can practice the skills critical to their own maximum performance. Your information technology (IT) managers, for example, could develop practice schedules for end-user technical support, desktop and network management, communications, and the various business applications they maintain. When some of the IT managers complain that they don't have enough time to work on the problems and projects they have, keep in mind that well-prepared IT managers might have avoided some of the problems they are now fixing. Make practice a part of your training priorities and see that it is done as scheduled.

Challenge other departments with the same kind of practice schedule. Practice is important for not only leaders and managers, but also all employees at all levels. Salespeople are notorious for acting as if they know everything, and chances are they will be reluctant to examine their abilities. Some short tests, however, will reveal skills and knowledge that need attention. Customer service clerks need to practice their skills in taking orders and handling complaints. Department managers need to practice their communications skills. Vice presidents need to practice their analysis and resource management skills.

The higher the rank, the more dramatic the consequences if leaders do not include practice as part of their preparation.

Practice Is Important at All Levels

Subordinates find it much easier to accomplish goals and follow orders if their leaders know what is needed and practice giving detailed and complete instructions. Over the years, you've likely been given very general directives without any of the information needed to complete the project. How often have you heard, "Go get more business," or "Cut costs"? When orders are this sketchy, you have to

Eight Things to Know About Your Competitors

1. **Products:** Which of your competitors' products are like your own? What are the features and benefits?
2. **People:** Who works for your competitors, and what are their backgrounds, qualifications, and personal motivations?
3. **Raw materials:** Who are your competitors' suppliers and what influences them?
4. **Strategies:** What are your competitors' current strategies and future goals?
5. **Customers:** Who do your competitors serve, and what is their share of the business?
6. **Strengths and weaknesses:** How well do you know the competing company and each department?
7. **Market influences:** What do your competitors control, and what is beyond their control?
8. **Prices and price influences:** Do you gather information and trends from several sources?

Eight Things to Know About Your Customers

1. **Their business:** What do they sell?
2. **Customers' customers:** Who are their customers, and what do they do with the products they buy?
3. **Concerns:** What are the concerns of your customers and of their customers?
4. **Use of products:** How your customers use your products, and what else do they buy?
5. **Raw materials and services:** What do your customers use, and what drives those markets?
6. **Their competitors:** Who are your customers' competitors, and who supplies them what they need? What are their strengths, weaknesses, and strategies?
7. **Market influences:** How much do you know about your customers' sales cycles, and what drives them and their suppliers?
8. **Key people, buyers, and influencers:** What do you know about the experience, personal goals, families, dreams and interests, and strengths and weaknesses of key persons?

make a lot of assumptions about the resources available and your range of authority. A thorough and complete set of instructions would certainly help reduce stress and get done what the boss wants.

If bosses are reluctant to practice giving better directives, you'll have to practice gathering more information. You don't want to ignore the directive or fail in reaching the goals, so it becomes your responsibility to make the assumptions and do what needs to be done. Since you understand the difficulty of operating with incomplete information, you can pass along your wisdom and give better directives to your subordinates.

One of the best ways for you to control stress is to prepare ahead of time for the inevitable attack. You can get ready for crises by practicing each scenario when everything is calm and under control. It wouldn't be hard for your vice president of sales or general sales manager to develop a practice exercise for competitive attacks or customer demands. Your company's top negotiator could just as easily set up a series of sessions to help frontline employees practice their negotiating skills.

Just as they prepare themselves, corporate leaders are also responsible for preparing employees for their jobs. When data-entry clerks make errors, for example, the department manager must take responsibility for the problems. There will be no errors if procedures are practiced and followed by employees who are properly trained and equipped. You as the leader get the credit for the good work and the bad. If you have employees who cannot learn the process for error-free work, you are responsible for replacing them with qualified people, but you cannot blame them for the problems they have created. Either you have failed to prepare them, or you have failed to replace them.

It isn't difficult for your company to identify the mistakes and problems that create stress. Some would say that closer supervision is needed, but if this is the solution, why hasn't your watchfulness already eliminated the problem? The answer lies in supervising the right activities—in preparing employees as well as their equipment and necessary tools.

Confidence in Yourself and Your Employees Helps Control Stress

The Army's demanding training gives soldiers a lot of confidence in themselves and their equipment—the tools they need to do the job. The positive stress of training helps soldiers achieve far more than they initially expect, and the pride of accomplishment reduces anxiety about upcoming challenges. The more GIs learn in both the classroom and live training exercises, the more certain they are that they can do the job.

For example, soldiers who are hesitant about operating high-powered weapons and heavy vehicles overcome their concern by practicing in increasingly difficult circumstances. The sergeants and

Eleven Things to Know About Technology

1. **Current technology:** Do you know what is used by your company, customers, competitors, and suppliers?
2. **Available technology:** Do you know what you should acquire in both equipment and knowledge?
3. **Aversions:** Are you making an effort to overcome any aversion to technology and learning how to adapt?
4. **Training:** What do you need to maximize use of technology and what training would help you, even if your company cannot pay your way?
5. **Contact management software:** Do you know how to use software like ACT! to keep up with the *who, what, when, where, how,* and *why* information?
6. **Communications:** Are you staying current with strategies for using e-mail and other electronic communications?
7. **Bridge lines:** Do you know how bridge lines can help you with customers and in-house coordination?
8. **Research tools:** Do you know how to use them and what to research?
9. **Collaboration tools:** Are you familiar with technology that can help you collaborate in-house, between divisions, and with industry experts, customers, and suppliers?
10. **Selling tools:** Do you know the tools available to you: audiovisual, electronic, printed, regular mail, and personal?
11. **Personal newsletters:** Do you know how to use these for communications and to build credibility?

officers teaching these technical courses are teachers, coaches, and mentors. No longer are they the demanding drill sergeants who taught the early lessons of discipline and obedience. These instructors instill a sense of pride and confidence that are critical for controlling stress and keeping these soldiers on their jobs at times of high risk.

The same shift in leadership is required in companies when employees switch from being trainees to being fully competent staff members. The coaching, mentorship, and confidence building are essential to their performance, especially as they confront obstacles and overcome challenges. Self-confidence is difficult to achieve if managers continue to make every decision and double-check every action.

If you have prepared your employees and given them sufficient practice, you must also have confidence in their ability and let them do their jobs. Employees need to know that they are part of the team and that their leaders support them. You can find out how you have been doing by simply asking your employees for their opinions. Most employees are bold enough to tell you what they think. If you respond in this area of leadership, you'll relieve a lot of stress and find employees working harder than expected, staying on the job longer, performing better, and being more enthusiastic about their work.

If you've been a demanding tyrant who holds control of every move, the shift to mentoring and coaching might be temporarily stressful for you. Regardless of how things have started out in your company, you can make the shift and let your team know that you support them. As you change your persona, there will be some lighthearted humor about the new you, but people will see that you truly want to support them. The lighthearted humor will pass, and the stress will decrease greatly for all of you. You can help your employees achieve far beyond their own level of confidence if you yourself are prepared and if you are willing to support them in their seemingly impossible tasks.

Chapter 7 continues this discussion about your leadership as it addresses the importance of teamwork for controlling workplace stress.

7

TEAMWORK AND STRESS MANAGEMENT

★

Unit Cohesiveness

Team building is the first item in the Army's list of actions that leaders can use to control combat stress reactions. The Army field manual FM 22-51, *Leaders' Manual for Combat Stress Control*, explains that "highly trained and cohesive units with good leadership have less than one (battle fatigue) casualty for every ten" soldiers wounded in action. The ratio for these cohesive units is much lower than that of one in five for medium-intensity combat or one in three for intense battles. Statistics such as these show the importance of establishing and maintaining cohesive units by developing soldier skills, trust, effective communications, and rigorous, realistic training.

Hard-Core Training

Combat realism integrated into the training enhances the team-building environment and prepares soldiers for the actual stress of combat. The U.S. Army Ranger School is one of the best in con-

Leadership Actions to Prevent Combat Stress Reactions

Build unit cohesion and unit pride—team building.
Help soldiers have stable home fronts.
Keep soldiers physically fit.
Conduct tough, realistic training.
Cross-train in key areas.
Enforce sleep discipline.
Plan for personal hygiene.
Preserve soldiers' welfare, safety, and health.
Reduce uncertainty.
Enforce individual preventive medicine measures.

From Army field manual FM 22-51, *Leaders' Manual for Combat Stress Control*

ducting realistic training to build unit cohesion. The training simulates warfare as soldiers are depleted physically, mentally, and emotionally. Rations are adequate but the physical demands of ranger school require a lot more food than is provided. Ranger students are hungry; some would even say starved. Students are tired, fatigued far beyond their expected ability to function. Rangers are pushed to the point of breaking. Each of these conditions fosters a sense of helping each other survive hardships, and completion of the tough training fosters bonding between the soldiers and cohesion in the unit.

Ranger buddies are assigned on the first day, and with the exception of individual proficiency testing, these two students are responsible for each other. If one of the two breaks the rules, both of them are in trouble. If one fails to overcome an obstacle, both of them repeat the effort. The ruggedness of the training and the hours spent together create a tight bond very quickly.

The teamwork of the ranger buddies then expands to include the entire platoon of approximately forty students. The rangers learn to count on every member of the team and to make sure every student succeeds. The training is so realistic that my own ranger class lost students to broken bones, fractured vertebrae, sprains, concussions, puncture wounds, near drownings, scorpion bites, snakebites, rope burns, and battle fatigue. The hazards involved in ranger training create such a cohesive team bonding that the team experiences sincere grief when members are injured and withdrawn from the course.

Ranger students are so tired that they learn to sleep while walking. Realistic dreams are common on forced marches. Soldiers have been known to wander out of formation when the unit was on the move, and when the *rescue* patrol found them, they had circled all the way back to the point of origin, unaware that they were not with the rest of the unit. The ranger students were astonished that not only could some students wander away from the main body, but also fatigue prevented the main body from realizing that these students were gone, until someone took a head count. Rangers learned that fatigue is an enemy, and when I later went into battle, I knew to be more careful with my troops.

Students were so hungry that they scrounged through the small dumps where previous students had disposed of C-ration cans. They hoped to find edible remnants or perhaps an unopened can. They learned the lore of harvesting what nature provided and ate things that would never be acceptable in civilized society. Eating trash left behind by others along with the bugs, berries, and plants kept the students going as physical stress took them beyond the limits of their endurance. Survival and success in accomplishing team objectives created bonding and unit cohesion similar to that generated by the rigors of combat.

The student leadership of these ranger units changes frequently to give everyone the opportunity to lead in simulated battle conditions and to test their ability to perform under extreme stress. As with all team efforts, everyone pulled together to make each student leader successful. One day they might be teaming up to help an exhausted ranger student complete a twenty-five-mile forced march, and the next day the revived student could be the leader. While students didn't want to admit it, they also knew they were all vulnerable to collapse and that everyone needed each other to get through the training.

Graduating from the U.S. Army Ranger School is one of the Army's highest achievements. A special shoulder patch is worn by all qualified U.S. Army Rangers, providing a visual display of the courage and skills of the soldier. Rangers know they can trust each other because of their shared experience and common character. The team bonding expands beyond the specific group that trained together and affects relationships among rangers wherever they encounter one another.

The extreme danger and simulated combat conditions increase the level of bonding for the soldiers, but a similar level of commitment exists among those who learn teamwork in much gentler conditions. In this chapter, you'll find some specific suggestions for developing the team spirit among your employees. You don't have to endanger their well-being to enhance their performance.

U.S. Army Airborne School

U.S. Army Airborne School is another of the Army's tough schools. The rigorous training lasts approximately three weeks and consists of physical conditioning, academic study, and practical jump experience.

As you might think, the first block of instruction consists of how to land once the soldiers have made that leap of faith from a perfectly good airplane. Hitting the ground, rolling with the fall, and controlling the parachute are technical skills that ensure a safe landing, but they are also extremely important in building the confidence of the paratrooper. These are primarily individual, rather than team, skills. Other soldiers in the training unit might provide encouragement, but each soldier has to learn how to make that landing.

Throughout the course of tough physical training, emphasis is on the teamwork involved. Many of the students need the help of others to complete the exhausting runs and physical training. Each soldier in the aircraft relies upon another to check their equipment when they stand up to make the jump. Teamwork is drilled into their minds as they learn about the extensive support system behind each jump—parachute packers, aircraft mechanics, pilots, meteorologists, jumpmasters, and pathfinders who go before them to mark the drop zone.

Every member of the unit learns that the team must succeed. The unit is to blame if a student doesn't complete a run with everyone else or doesn't learn every subject. The combination of intensive training, personal danger, and unit accomplishment builds a tremendous sense of esprit de corps and team pride in being airborne troopers. The teamwork is far more than a simple tradition among airborne soldiers; it is essential for the success of combat operations where individual or team failure can mean death or capture by the enemy. The special set of silver wings pinned to the soldier's uniform tells everyone of this trooper's bravery and achievement.

Civilian corporations seldom face the dramatic training regimen of the Army's elite troops, but there are some similarities that illustrate the importance of these team building efforts.

Corporate Team Building

Some civilian organizations have uniforms and insignia that recognize individual achievement. Law enforcement officers' and firefighters' uniforms are easily recognized. Unique shirts, jackets, vests, and caps identify employees who belong to other special groups. Printed T-shirts, buttons, badges, and corporate ID tags are evident wherever you travel.

Some of the bonding is so great that people wear the articles and badges when they are *off duty* or long after their departure from the team itself. Corporations recognize the team accomplishments with graduation certificates, plaques, mugs, and other items to brand the team and compliment the individuals. You probably have some of these same traditions in your own company, but if you're looking for ideas you might try the following:

- Develop logo mugs, caps, shirts, or sweaters for each department. You can do this annually to keep the items fresh, but you'll defeat your purpose if you buy cheap stuff.
- Provide a logo item to special task force or problem-solving team members upon completion of the project.
- Sponsor a team night out, in recognition of a special achievement or as an annual affair to encourage team bonding

and relationships. People don't really have time on the job for this type of bonding. Be sure to give corporate gifts at these events.

- Establish athletic teams to compete with other departments. You pay the space expenses and maybe even the equipment costs. Many corporate problems can be solved by getting team members to compete together.
- Present special training for team members to enhance job performance and team relationships.
- Send key team members for high-adventure training where the physical excitement encourages bonding.
- Sponsor an annual company picnic where teams participate in a unique way to provide food, entertainment, or athletic competition.
- Generate internal competition so departments compete for the best overall improvement or the fewest quality complaints. Be careful not to have internal teams competing for cash rewards such as annual bonuses, or you'll create a lot of negative stress and distrust that is hard to repair.

Your investment in team awards or recognition items will be returned many times over through decreased stress, improved performance, and decreased absenteeism. You will want to budget for these items and make sure the funds are available. When times get tough, you still want to keep these programs going. Encouraging teamwork in tough times is more important than during good times, so keep these awards going, even if you have to downsize the awards because of financial concerns.

The value the Army places on teamwork and stress control can be seen in the five-year, $26 million contract awarded to innovative solutions provider Dynamics Research Corporation (DRC) to develop a program for increasing teamwork and effectiveness for aircrews and medical teams. The cost of the program will be balanced against greater efficiency and saved lives. Confidence in their program is high because DRC has proven their concepts in both civilian hospitals and the Army.[1]

Corporate Crises—Weak Versus Strong Teams

Corporate leaders who have weathered financial crises know very well how their teams react to the stressors of plant closings, management restructuring, reduction of personnel, hiring freezes, payroll reductions, shifts in production schedules, changes in quality, and the numerous other strategies implemented for corporate survival.

If team members are lost through layoffs and terminations, you need to meet with the remaining team members and explain the circumstances of the departure. Consult with your human resources leaders or general counsel about what should be said. If several people are terminated at the same time, be sure to explain the company's financial circumstances or restructuring goals and let the remaining team members know whether there will be more terminations. Those who remain behind suffer from negative stress reactions. Employees working in a strong team environment grieve the loss of team members, but the esprit de corps and the sense of duty that made their team strong will also carry them through the anger, guilt, and grief.

If death has caused the loss, you can help control stress and set the stage for ongoing team operations by doing the following:

- Allow the remaining team members to talk openly about the death.
- Acknowledge the individual's contributions openly.
- Explain that you, too, feel the loss and understand what it means to family members.
- Display a sense of confidence about carrying on with your mission.
- Guide employees in promptly resuming meaningful work.
- Send flowers or other requested memorial gifts and attend the funeral.
- Arrange a memorial ceremony at your company or another suitable site for those who cannot attend the funeral.
- Write a letter to the family explaining how much the person meant to your company.

- Remember that your actions are as much for those left behind as for those who died.

The stronger the corporate team, the stronger their response during crises. As with Army units, teams with low unit cohesion suffer more than those with a strong sense of team membership. It goes without saying that it is easier to work on team cohesion and esprit before the crises, which are just around the corner.

Developing Teamwork

The concepts of Army training are useful to corporations who have long used team building as part of their everyday operations. Young managers are assigned team projects and thrown together to overcome obstacles. Seasoned professionals raise the stress level in various departments and require team performance as part of the stress inoculation process.

The crises that face leaders in the office, on the production floor, and in the field require the leaders to work together to overcome various threats. Long hours and grueling schedules create a bond among those who succeed. Stories of these episodes endure for years and become part of the corporate lore.

Some companies are adventurous in their Army-like team-building activities. Companies like Bank One, IBM, KPMG, Kraft, Eli Lilly, Pizza Hut, Roche, and Shell contract with adventure training companies to enhance the skills and bonding of some teams. The training companies they use specialize in specific types of adventures such as canoeing, climbing, ropes courses, cross-country navigation, skiing, and wilderness trekking.

The goal of this type of training is to accelerate the bonding and cohesion, similar to what soldiers experience as they complete rigorous adventure training. There are many opportunities across the United States, as well as some exotic locations worldwide, to serve your company leaders. Be sure to check the references before contracting with such an organization. Some of them are better equipped and get better results than others.

Ten Ways to Prepare Leaders and Teams to Meet Stressors Head-On

In addition to the Army's realistic combat training and the corporate adventure training, a number of simpler methods can prepare teams for the stressors they will encounter. The following techniques are not listed in order of importance, so you can choose the ones that fit your company's needs. If team-building strategies such as these are new to your company, I suggest you work with only one or two strategies at a time until your teams get used to the new working environment.

You can explain your intentions for increased team-building performance, or you can simply advise everyone that you have some new strategies you will implement. You will receive many complaints either way, so you have to determine your priorities and set your resolve if you want to raise your team cohesion and benefit from the increased performance and stress control. You might engage a training consultant or brainstorm internally to come up with some variations on these concepts.

1. **Implement a series of deadlines for leaders and employees.** If your people are accustomed to working on open-ended projects or never actually meeting established deadlines, your change of course will cause team members to work together and increase the pressure to perform on schedule. Army commanders frequently increase positive stress and team-building participation by asking for projects to be done well ahead of the established deadline.

2. **Announce increased performance expectations in every area.** The positive stress that comes with this type of announcement might even cause some employees to seek jobs elsewhere, giving you the opportunity to hire someone who comes in expecting to meet a higher standard. Employees who accept the challenge will feel better about their accomplishment, and morale will increase. Most Army situations prevent soldiers from simply quitting their jobs, so military leaders have an even greater challenge in motivating people to perform according to new standards.

3. **Increase the frequency of personnel reviews to highlight areas for improvement, addressing all deficiencies, large and small.** A quarterly analysis of strengths, weaknesses, and performance goals helps team members understand whether they are meeting your expectations.

4. **Create ever-increasing expectations for those who perform well.** You do your high achievers a favor if you keep raising the bar. Many people need the added challenge to perform their best, and they will appreciate your confidence and encouragement in reaching new heights.

5. **Develop a list of necessary improvements, and assign teams to achieve each.** People want to contribute to the success of the organization, and these projects increase team involvement. Employees will see the difference they make, and appreciate the bonding that occurs on their team. The Army does this by assigning tougher and tougher missions that contribute to the unit's overall combat readiness level.

6. **Allow teams to compete against each other to achieve objectives.** As with Army leaders, you'll find that individuals and teams appreciate the competitive arrangements and work hard to reach their goals. The efforts of team members working together will improve their teamwork and build esprit, strengthening their performance in other areas.

7. **Implement mandatory off-site social events—attendance is not for entertainment but for team building and team bonding.** You don't need to advertise these events as team-building exercises, but they will have that effect. You may need to schedule these events during work hours to maximize attendance, or use your special leadership ability to get the participation of two-income families whose hectic schedules sometimes conflict with what you want to do. Army leaders schedule quarterly and annual events, and all attendees have to pay their share. If you make the events attractive enough, they will come.

8. **Provide challenging team-confidence builders both in-house and off-site.** You can schedule your own mini-adventure training

exercises at your business or at the local go-cart track, climbing wall, ropes course, bowling alley, or high-school track. Your public library and the World Wide Web have several good resources on the subject of team building, and your human resources managers will be glad to assist in setting up some of these confidence builders. Even if some employees are limited by physical conditions, schedule the adventure training and give these people significant responsibilities as part of the outing. The more your teams work together on these types of events, the better they will perform and the better they will control the stress of everyday corporate work.

9. **Personally monitor and be involved in the progress of significant team assignments.** Army leaders establish reporting schedules to make sure tasks are moving in the right direction and that teams meet intermediate deadlines. You can use these meetings or inspections to contribute your own ideas and to praise the team for what they have achieved.

10. **Publicly recognize those who perform well (and raise the level of expectation again).** Regardless of what anyone says about the need for public recognition, it will serve you well in your team-building efforts. Some people might not need as much recognition as others, but everyone likes being appreciated. If some truly do object, help them understand that their involvement will be an encouragement to others. As discussed earlier in this book, the Army uses a variety of memos, letters, awards, and medals to recognize achievement. The more team recognition you can provide, the more your employees understand their contribution to the company and the more meaningful their work becomes.

11. **Bonus team-building action: increase team bonding by awarding members with recognizable apparel, plaques, pins, and so on.** In the spirit of giving more than is promised, here is an eleventh idea for you to consider. Don't award anything cheap, or it will devalue its meaningfulness. As mentioned previously, these awards contribute significantly to the team-building effort and demonstrate your appreciation for your employees' work.

Strategies such as these prepare both leaders and teams for the stressors that await them. Preparing to confront stress is somewhat like weight training. Even the small weights used by beginners cause them trouble. The weights get heavy fast and muscles are sore for days. But frequent repetition adds strength and endurance. Soon the lifter looks forward to the exercise, and the stronger muscles no longer complain. It's the same with stress conditioning for teams. Raise the level of stress slowly, and your team will soon find themselves prepared to confront significant stressors.

If you already use some of these strategies, you can increase team-building effectiveness by adding another from the list. Whatever you do will put you ahead of the competition because they are simply not focused on their team building. You'll be far ahead of those companies who do nothing more than use the word *team building* in their advertising. Weaker organizations need to select one of the stress-building strategies and build on it to strengthen the entire organization. It isn't too late to make a plan and prepare teams for the stressors they will encounter.

The earlier list of ten team-building strategies is a starter kit for your own ideas or for adapting these ideas to fit your own policies and procedures. Your leaders and team members will go beyond those listed, and your better team members will embrace the challenge with enthusiasm.

During this time of training, some team members might be unwilling to undergo the increased stress. If some are unable or unwilling to help prepare the team for the future, they will certainly fail the team during a crisis. It is better to find out early how they perform and consider alternatives for the individuals and for the company.

Top Ten Obstacles to Successful Teamwork

Some leaders build teamwork as naturally as they breathe, but others have to work at it. When corporate leaders lack the ability or confidence, they often contract with consultants to provide team-building exercises and seminars. The sad thing is that many of those who purchase these team-building packages fail to correct some of the underlying problems, and thus waste their team-building efforts. These obstacles to successful teamwork may seem like common sense to some people, but the obstacles are less obvious to those causing the problems. Maybe you should take counsel with a trusted friend to find out if you are guilty of any of the following:

1. **Ego—too much me.** When someone's ego gets in the way of team performance, Army leaders are quick to point this out and coach individuals into a team mind-set.

2. **Absence of a servant's heart.** Some commanders are very direct in explaining things to subordinates, but most Army leaders perform as servants to others on their team, helping, coaching, and encouraging the completion of the unit mission.

3. **Lack of appreciation for what is done.** There are occasions when Army leaders and team members fail to demonstrate their appreciation, but Army training and peer involvement encourage all leaders to appreciate how the teamwork contributes to their success.

4. **Inadequate recognition for being a team player (group and individual rewards).** This obstacle can ruin the team's effectiveness, so it is important for you to follow the Army's example of publicly recognizing individual and team contributions.

5. **Failure to communicate.** Overcoming this obstacle can be achieved with the Army's method of establishing intermediate deadlines and reports. It is as important for you to communicate with the team as it is for them to communicate up the chain of command.

6. **Failure to understand importance of team approach.** Very few Army leaders fail to understand the importance of a team approach, but they must constantly reinforce this concept with soldiers who are still in the learning process. Your personal communication will go far in helping all team members understand their individual roles as well as that of their team.

7. **Absence of proper tools to get the job done.** It is unlikely that teams will succeed if they lack the tools and resources to achieve their

assigned task. This is where your servant leadership can help them get what is needed or to find some alternative that will permit mission success.

8. **Inadequate understanding of upstream and downstream procedures and processes.** Poor understanding of the processes surrounding their effort limits the effectiveness of a team. Army leaders are careful to educate team members or provide the resources necessary in this regard.

9. **Inadequate understanding of organizational goals.** Because it is difficult for teams to achieve when they don't understand the organizational goals, Army leaders comment on the mission or objective in each meeting on the subject. Chapter 4 showed how a restatement of the mission is the first step in every AAR.

10. **Lack of management support for team.** This is probably the biggest cause of team failure. Army leaders overcome this obstacle by acting as members of the team, showing up during the process, participating as requested by the team or as determined necessary, and supporting the team as needed during each phase of the work.

Team members can tell you why the team is having problems, but critical self-analysis is required to recognize these obstacles in yourself. Listen to the team. Strong teams help reduce stress and increase productivity. They help achieve in the face of great odds. Regardless of the team-building stage in your company, employees can also improve performance and reduce stress by practicing their skills until they become automatic reactions. Chapter 8 picks up on teamwork and shows how practice can get you ready for the daily grind or your next big event.

Notes

1. Dynamics Research Corporation news release, 2001.

8

PRACTICE

★

In combat, the only way to survive an ambush is to return fire immediately and run through the enemy shooters. The concept is that the enemy must take cover from your gunfire, and some of you will be able to run right through their position and out the other side.

Running through the fire is an easy thing to describe. It takes less than a minute to explain the whole process, but when you're being shot at and your friends are collapsing around you, it's pretty tough to run right into the teeth of the enemy. This encounter with the enemy is so deadly that your response has to be immediate and automatic. There is no time to think about what must be done, and turning away from the danger is not an option. You must practice running through the fire until it becomes a matter of instinct.

What do you do when you're ambushed by life? Have you trained yourself to respond when you're ambushed by your competitors? Do you know how you'll survive the ambush of illness, family crisis, death of loved ones, or financial upset? Just as with the Army's ground troops, it isn't a matter of whether you'll be ambushed; it's a matter of when. If you knew when the attacks were coming, they wouldn't be called ambushes. If you're not ready when the time comes, you might not survive.

So back to the question: What are you doing to get ready for the ambushes in life? Have you made a plan? Did you practice your response? Are you ready? This chapter teaches you how to practice so you are ready for *every* situation.

Corporate Ambushes

Ambushes happen in the corporate world all the time. The mid-1980s' pesticide leak that killed 5,000 people in Bhopal, India, was certainly an ambush for Union Carbide. Critics say that Union Carbide abandoned the plant after compensating victims' families $200–$500 each for a total of $470 million. Critics accuse Union Carbide and its current owner, Dow Chemical, of contaminating the groundwater by failing to clean up the site, and thus contributing to the deaths of another 15,000 people.

Dow Chemical has been candid in explaining that because of the liability situations that would arise, they cannot openly admit responsibility or pay for cleanup at this time. Some analysts say that this issue continues to affect the value of Dow Chemical stock and that failure to embrace the danger in this ambush has led to a twenty-year problem for these companies.

Also in the early 1980s, Johnson & Johnson (J&J) was twice ambushed by a terrorist poisoning of many bottles of Extra Strength Tylenol in the Chicago area, killing several customers. The first incidence cost the company over a billion dollars because customers lost confidence in the company. When the second incident occurred a couple of years later, J&J embraced the danger and confronted the problem head-on. An immediate nationwide recall took the remaining inventory off the shelves, and within weeks J&J's openness about the problem rebuilt public trust, putting the product back in the running as America's favored pain reliever.

Along with J&J, the U.S. Food and Drug Administration issued requirements for tamper-evident (T-E) packaging on all pharmaceuticals. The food industry followed with T-E packaging. Such a rapid response by bureaucracies like these is unexpected, but in this situation they embraced the danger in ambush—they took action immediately.

Some companies, however, had no practice in dealing with disasters and crumbled when ambushed. When Bridgestone-Firestone's faulty tires caused a number of fatal accidents, the company's delayed response led to a second ambush; the faulty tires ambushed them first, but their defensive posturing ambushed them again. Not until the company confronted mounting lawsuits did they finally initiate a recall of millions of tires from across the world. They might eventually survive this double ambush, but it's costing them much more money than if they had immediately embraced the danger the way J&J did.

Companies don't have to wait for an ambush to decide what they will do. These decisions can be made ahead of time to preclude the emotional involvement in the midst of the crisis. Moreover, corporate leaders are responsible for creating these policies and practicing their implementation. Every responsible company—and leader—needs to do a risk assessment, develop appropriate and ethical responses, and practice just how they will react when they are ambushed. Shelving assessments and policies does little for reducing risk, and the lack of practice does nothing for controlling stress.

At the other end of the spectrum is Texas Instruments (TI) and their efforts to avoid ambushes by using risk assessment and response planning. TI's stated goal is zero accidents, zero waste, and zero illness, and they have reaped big rewards by dealing with the situations uncovered with operational and administrative risk assessments. The company has saved millions of dollars by analyzing each area and finding risky activities and overlooked follow-up requirements.

You can implement similar procedures in your own company by reviewing operating procedures and safeguards in each department. Practicing established procedures and contingency plans can reveal errors, necessary changes, and alternatives that were unavailable when the plan was written. Hiring an outside consultant will more than pay for itself, because the consultant's perspective will be objective and based upon observations in other industries. If your company is not ready to invest in a full program the way TI tackled the problem, you can start with your own division or department. You won't go wrong.

A company where safety and good business practices prevail has much less stress—not to mention its valuable gain of improved productivity, increased profits, and fewer ambushes.

How Corporations Can Practice

Everybody knows how to exit a building in a time of crisis, right? Actually, unannounced fire drills usually reveal some shortcomings as people pause to finish certain tasks, gather up personal items, or travel improper exit paths. In my own experience, I've even discovered blocked exits, chained doors, and employees who stayed behind because they "had too much work to do." If it has been a while since you practiced your company's emergency plans, you might be surprised at how inadequate or outdated the plan has become.

After the terrorist attacks on the Pentagon and the World Trade Center, companies across the United States required emergency exit drills. Everyone wanted to practice these safety precautions, but some companies have let these drills slide, doing only the minimum required by law. Has your company continued the drills and implemented the improvements needed?

Risk-attentive companies also have drills for storms, earthquakes, and other natural disasters. And others develop written procedures and practice their response to anticipated operational ambushes such as electrical failures, computer crashes, public relations disasters, equipment malfunctions, and transportation delays.

Businesses should practice their desired reactions to a wide range of ambushes—financial, administrative, information technology, operations, customer service, public relations, advertising, and marketing. As discussed later in this chapter, the Army tests plans and strategies with war games. Frequently, problems are identified and corrections are made to the training and procedures for each type of operation.

Another way to practice surviving ambushes is through analysis of individual competency. This means testing technical and leadership competence of people who run the organization—a rare practice in most companies. The Army requires continuous training of individuals and units. Notice the word *continuous*. Year in and year out, units are tested against standards for combat or operational readiness.

At every level, commanders require their units to practice and prepare for scheduled tests. Officers of every rank and sergeants throughout the Army find these training exercises valuable, and soldiers rehearse over and over what will be required in the unit test. In spite of the practice and preparation, many units are found lacking in some critical expertise when the test adds another level of realism and objective outsiders evaluate their performance.

Is your company this aggressive in training people to perform in all areas of their responsibilities? Do you have a training schedule, or do you only respond when something causes problems? Does your human resources department have enough leverage to make sure everyone—leaders included—*successfully* completes scheduled training?

The Army war-gaming used to test knowledge and ability has a lot of value. As an aide-de-camp for Major General George S. Patton Jr. (son of the famed World War II general) I was privileged to observe his supervision of an Armor School war game at Fort Knox, Kentucky. The exercise involved no troops or mobile equipment but tested the planning and support capabilities of battalion staff officers in a simulated tactical operations center (TOC).

In a manner reminiscent of old Blood and Guts Patton, General Patton stepped into the TOC and asked the operations officer how much tank ammunition he had planned for the upcoming battle. The officer confidently reported the planned rate of expenditure, current inventory, and how much he planned to move forward from division supply. The officer had performed well in responsible positions for many years and answered with the textbook solution for this question. He thought he was doing well until General Patton asked him the follow-up question: "How many operational 5-ton trucks do you have?"

Promptly, the officer quoted the number of trucks assigned to the command, but when pressed, he admitted that he didn't know how many were operational and how many were out of service for maintenance.

Without hesitation, General Patton responded. "A private can count ammo, sir. You're responsible for having enough ammunition and for getting it to the front, but you have no idea whether you have the trucks to haul it. We need leaders who know the entire process. You're relieved of your job here!"

The officer was stunned to be relieved in the middle of the war game. His career wasn't affected by the relief, but it sure got his attention—and the attention of everyone else in the command post. There was silence in the room as General Patton slapped his leather gloves against the palm of his hand and made a teaching point to the rest of the staff: "The book solution doesn't win wars. You have to think, and you have to *practice*."

Army war games evaluate technical skills, analytical ability, and emotional control as participants come under pressure to perform well. Use of observers and AARs such as those described in Chapter 4 capture details and improve performance on subsequent tests and under fire.

Similar war games are rare in corporate training, when they should be required. The term *war game* might seem daunting, but in actuality, the games are simply graded practice exercises that include all of the people who would be involved if the scenario were real.

Good human resource directors and other leaders in the company can plan training exercises. You can get as elaborate as you want, testing expertise in conversation around a conference table or conducting multilevel tests over a period of several days. Corporate leaders lay out the assumptions and describe the situations they want analyzed, and the company responds as though they had actually encountered the problem or opportunity. Examples of corporate war games could include things such as increased order size, customer complaints, computer network failures, sabotage, Occupational Safety and Health Administration (OSHA) findings, public relations disasters, and so on.

Such corporate war games can uncover problems you have with current operating procedures, levels of expertise and understanding, contingency plans, and other capabilities. As in the Army, corporate war games can help leaders understand readiness levels and errors that need attention. The effort will pay off in team bonding, reduced stress, and improved readiness.

If your company isn't already using hands-on practice, here are the steps to implement such a process. Start with a brainstorming session. Your team will easily develop a list of what your company needs to practice as you ask them to discuss.

1. What is it we want to do—what are our goals?
2. Where are we now—how far do we have to go?
3. What are our strengths—that is, a realistic evaluation?
4. What are our weaknesses, without pulling any punches?
5. What equipment, training, and personnel are needed—what are the maximum benefit and minimum expense?
6. What risks do we face in reaching our goals, both internal and external?

These brainstorming sessions aren't for the timid. You need top management present, and they need to encourage open and frank discussion. If the honchos speak up, they need to make sure their remarks are encouraging and not limiting to other participants.

Practice Through Inspections

At one point in my Army career, I was assigned as an inspector general at Fort Knox, acting as the eyes and ears of the commanding general. Our task included taking complaints and conducting preliminary investigations, but the most public function was conducting the required annual readiness inspection for all units on post. Almost every unit dreaded these detailed inspections, but preparing for the event gave commanders another team-building experience as the unit reviewed, updated, and made current every conceivable aspect of their mission readiness—equipment, personnel records, administration, training, food service, safety, weapons, and so on.

The inspections generated a lot of positive stress, of course, but no more so than the annual corporate audits conducted for publicly held companies. Corporate audits are similar to Army inspections, but the audits are oriented toward generally accepted accounting procedures rather than operational performance, unless it has an impact on the financial report.

In addition to the annual financial audit, more aggressive companies also schedule team visits for special areas of interest such as accounting of controlled substances, spot-checking inventory accuracy, and safety audits. Some companies beef up the audits with scheduled refresher training for new products and procedures. Those who actually inspect for operational readiness can ensure that employees and individual divisions are ready for the ambushes they will encounter in the marketplace

As you read the following Army illustrations, you may worry that your employees will say things like "This is a business. You can't run it like the Army." or "We do this stuff everyday. We don't have to be tested." Similar remarks can be heard throughout the Army as well. "This is the Army. You can't run it like a business." Reality is that business principles must be used in the Army to make sure things run properly, and there is nothing wrong with using Army techniques to make sure businesses maximize their success.

As the inspector general at Fort Knox, I found that commanders sometimes failed because they put on blinders and refused to learn good business practices that would have helped them succeed. Some of the units I inspected truly could have benefited from a good understanding of inventory control, personnel management, scheduled maintenance, and other highly developed corporate practices.

Similar points can be made from my corporate experience, where I observed that businesses can learn from successful Army procedures, such as practicing and rehearsing reactions to ambushes. For example, salespeople should be more than willing to practice one-on-one or in groups for the sales presentations that determine the fate of companies. Role-playing, answering aloud the anticipated objections and questions, and responding to customer needs can all be a part of the routine. Negotiation practice gives salespeople and managers more confidence and a significant advantage when they go head-to-head with savvy buyers. You can bet the buyers are practicing their negotiating skills.

Likewise, operations managers can practice to achieve improved performance, reduced waste, more accurate inventory accountability, energy conservation, enhanced scheduling, automated quality management, and along with everyone else, better people skills. Good operations managers can think of dozens of areas that need practice within their departments and in competition with others.

Professional customer service employees can role-play answering objections as well as practice such day-to-day activities as accurate product knowledge, customer response time, order entry, and company awareness. On one occasion, I surprised my sales team by asking them to identify all of the company's products that would serve a specific client need. Very few of the salespeople could give a complete answer, and on some of the applications, the entire team together failed to identify all of the products that would meet the customer's needs. No wonder stress levels were so high. We didn't know our products, and we didn't practice rapid recall.

Accounting and finance departments can practice items such as information retrieval, invoicing accuracy, management of outstanding receivables, collection of overdue invoices, credit risk analysis, reporting information to the feds, and tax implications. All the efforts to buy smart, sell more, and lower production costs are wasted without superior financial management.

Because day-to-day business experiences are less dramatic than Army ambushes, the training can be less dramatic as well. Leave the blank ammunition and explosives out of it, but bring in the questions and performance objectives that test the preparedness of leaders, managers, and employees in every department. Just like the ambush training, it will take time to learn how to practice and even more time to develop the skills. Here are some specific actions you can take to get things started:

- Asking prepared questions over a period of time will help determine whether skills and readiness meet your standards. One way to probe in depth is to ask the question *why* five times for every situation. Don't accept the first *excuse*; drill to the core and find out the reasons.
- Site visits with specific observations in mind will give you an understanding of staff capabilities. Experience shows that these visits have to be frequent and repetitive for you to see what is actually going on rather than what you expect to see.
- Organized test events will hone everyone's performance and readiness for the common events that can be expected in business. You, too, will be better prepared as you practice developing the tests.

- Actual implementation of contingency plans will reveal both strengths and weaknesses in the plans. You will have plenty of opportunities to improve both plans and performance. You might be surprised at how out-of-date some of the plans are.
- Testing will improve performance under fire and reduce the possibility of extreme stress reactions in case of the real event. Your own stress level will be reduced as you gain confidence in your team's performance and readiness.
- Positive stress can be used to improve responses. Practicing and testing will harden employees for the stress they'll find in a crisis and reduce negative stress responses.

If professional athletes, actors, and musicians find it necessary to practice every day, it is realistic to expect practice among people with other skills and talents. Several years' experience should not reduce the need for practice. Instead, the more experienced a person becomes, the more he or she should recognize the need to practice.

Continuous learning and practice can increase stress endurance and prepare people for action in the toughest situations. In Chapter 9, you'll learn just how the Army faces tough times with success.

9

THE ULTIMATE TEST

★

Resilience is the "ability to recover quickly from illness, change, or misfortune."

—AMERICAN HERITAGE DICTIONARY, FOURTH EDITION, 2000

An electric power outage brought eight northeastern states to a standstill at 4:15 p.m. on Thursday, August 14, 2003. Every home, business, factory, restaurant, theme park, traffic light, and radio and TV station experienced the blackout. Estimates of the damage ran in excess of $5 billion.

While some of these businesses and homes were without electricity for days, others were resilient enough to be back in operation within a very short time. The largest supermarket chain, Kroger, remained closed the following day while regional grocery and department store operator, Meijer, was open for business within a couple of hours, using generators to meet electrical needs. About three-fourths of the darkened Wal-Mart stores had reopened by midday on Friday along with all of the Home Depot stores. Wall Street's New York Stock Exchange made a big deal out of ringing its opening bell at 9:30 a.m. Friday morning, while air-conditioning problems delayed the opening of the American Stock Exchange.

Some businesses had a very difficult time getting back on their feet. More than thirty-five of Ford and GM's parts and assembly plants were still closed on Friday morning; across the country, manufactur-

ing that depended on service from the closed operations felt the rip-
pling effect. Most branch banks remained closed, even if they had
generators, because they couldn't connect with parent-bank comput-
ers. One branch bank in Michigan reported closing because city services were still unavailable. Many businesses took the next day as a
holiday and went into the weekend hoping electricity would return
before Monday morning. Every airline flight scheduled into and out
of the affected area was postponed. Amtrak between Washington,
D.C., and New York City was out of commission. Local governments
did what they could to alleviate the problem for commuters and trav-
elers, but the increased bus service and suspension of tolls didn't do
much for the thousands of stranded people.

After the blackout, Long Island Power Authority provided customers with ideas on how to conserve power and avoid additional
outages once they were back online. The list might have reduced the
risk of another outage, but it did little in building the resiliency of
businesses for future outages.

The resilient companies operated on backup generators as did hospitals, nuclear plants, NASDAQ, Verizon, AT&T, Internet providers,
and police departments. Some of the resilient businesses had learned
how to cope with electric power interruptions from the rolling black-
outs of the 1990s in California. During the widespread power outages in California, San Diego Gas & Electric contributed to the
strength and resiliency of their customers by publishing a checklist
of approximately seventy-five things to be accomplished before, during, and after a power outage to prepare corporate buildings, employees, and equipment. Companies in the Northeast who learned from
the California experience and took these countermeasures seriously
were ready with contingency plans. Those who didn't prepare for such
problems lacked resiliency and could not rebound as quickly. The
result: their businesses didn't hold up when faced with a real test.

Individuals and businesses encounter illness, change, and misfortune on a daily basis. The resilient ones rely upon solid preparation,
quick thinking, and flexible adaptation to keep going in the face of
adversity. This chapter examines how the Army stays resilient in the
toughest situations and shows how you and your business can, too.

Resiliency in Time of War

The same ability to overcome change and misfortune could be seen in the Union forces deployed to defend Baltimore and Washington, D.C., during the American Civil War. General George Meade and his staff had developed a sound plan for defending the cities against the Confederate forces, who were known to be moving northward through the Shenandoah Valley. The plan of defense included terrain well suited for this purpose, sufficient troops, and a good system of resupply for ammunition and other items.

Federal forces looking for the enemy encountered a small number of them at Gettysburg, Pennsylvania, as the tired and poorly equipped Southerners scouted the town for shoes. When a larger Confederate unit attacked to rescue the foraging troops, the Union soldiers broke contact and established a defensive position on the nearby high ground to await reinforcements.

General Robert E. Lee reinforced the Confederate unit attacking the heights, and when the Union Army brought in their own reinforcements, General Lee decided to reorient his entire army and engage the enemy at Gettysburg instead of farther east.

General Meade went into action and ordered troops to march all night to help those defending the ridge above Gettysburg. Within approximately twenty-four hours, General Meade had redeployed more than a hundred thousand troops along with more than 350 cannons and a strong reserve force that he could send into action as needed. The Confederates faced this formidable force with only roughly sixty-two thousand soldiers, less than half the opponent's number of cannons, and no reserve.

The battle continued into day three with Confederates attacking across open wheat fields and the Union defending from an exposed rocky ridgeline. By the end of day three, the Union Army claimed victory. The total number of Union and Confederate soldiers killed, wounded, captured, and missing was approximately 51,000, making it the greatest land battle ever fought in the Western Hemisphere.

The resiliency of the Union army can be seen in their flexibility to meet the enemy at Gettysburg even though the large and cumbersome force had been deployed elsewhere. Their hasty night marches and movement of supplies avoided a defeat that would have given the Confederates a significant psychological advantage in their march on Washington. The resilient Union Army displaced soldiers quickly and developed an alternative defensive plan while on the move, bringing success to what otherwise would have had a much different outcome, for both the battle and the war.

Corporate Battles

As in the military, corporate victors are the companies who survive the battle and live to fight another day. The corporate losers are just that—losers. They go out of business, taking with them investments and jobs. The winners in the military and corporate battles generally are seen as resilient because of their perseverance and successful use of resources. The losers might persevere, but their errors in the areas of judgment, use of resources, and defensive strategy reveal shortcomings.

Two companies that illustrate this difference are Chrysler and Studebaker. Both companies were well established and had long histories of overcoming obstacles, but serious financial difficulties showed only one of them to be resilient. Studebaker found themselves unable to compete with larger manufacturers and imports, and finally they went out of business. Chrysler, on the other hand, fought for government loans, developed new products, fired up their marketing efforts, and survived to become one of America's most respected corporations. Chrysler's resiliency helped them reestablish a healthy business while employing thousands of Americans.

Companies are involved in this battle for survival on a daily basis. Those who survive are the companies who can adapt to the changing market, incorporate new products, and keep up with technology. They are resilient.

Resiliency Versus Anticipation

Both Studebaker and Chrysler were surprised by the situations they faced, but the victors were better prepared for the encounter. Aaron

Wildavsky, author of *Searching for Safety*, says that resiliency is something greater than simply planning for what can go wrong. He describes traditional risk management as being *anticipation*, where someone figures out what can go wrong and plans for it. *Resiliency*, on the other hand, is the quality that helps companies rebound when the unexpected occurs.[1]

Looking back at the Battle of Gettysburg, neither army knew exactly where they would engage the enemy, but both sides practiced their marksmanship, exercised their canons, trained for tactical maneuvers, developed their communication systems, and filled the pipeline with food and ammunition. When the two armies met, both used their physical resources as they were prepared to do, but the Union Army proved to be more resilient in responding to the threat, gauging what the enemy would do, and maneuvering their own units accordingly. While both armies did what was anticipated, the victory went to the Union Army as they responded well to the surprises they encountered.

The same can be true in your own company. You will be the victor when you react well to the unexpected, and the following section reveals the Army's four ways to boost resiliency.

Four Ways the Army Strengthens Resiliency

The Army recognizes there is more to victory than technical skills and determination. Of course, competency and determination are important, but these qualities alone do not ensure success where continuous combat operations and adverse conditions can degrade performance. If soldiers are going to perform well in these conditions, they need to be resilient and ready to spring back from whatever obstacle or unexpected situation they encounter. Army field manual FM 6-22.5, *Combat Stress*, addresses four specific measures "that must be introduced prior to combat" to "slow the rate of performance degradation" and ensure success.[2] Measures that commanders must include are in the areas of safety, food intake, combat load, and physical fitness, all of which can be effective for building resiliency in your company.

The Importance of Safety in Sustaining Resiliency

Both corporate and military leaders are concerned about the safety of their people. *Combat Stress* explains that accident rates increase 50 percent after 72 hours of continuous combat, because by then a strong tendency to take shortcuts develops.[3]

Military leaders are taught to schedule rest periods during strenuous operations. They know to prepare formal sleep schedules for themselves and their soldiers when continuous operations cause loss of sleep. When sleep deprivation or physical fatigue cannot be avoided, Army leaders give additional emphasis to safety precautions. Troops are reminded to engage the safety lock on their weapons to avoid accidentally firing. Frequent counts are taken to make sure that no one has dropped out of formation. Drivers often switch responsibilities with others to avoid vehicle accidents. Partners double-check each other's work and weapons to avoid fatigue-related mistakes.

However, fatigue shortcuts a person's thinking, and some tragic accidents occur in spite of everyone's efforts, especially where weapons and heavy equipment are involved. One young lieutenant I visited at the Fort Knox Ireland Army Hospital had an arm amputated because he reached through an opening inside a tank for a map just as another student rotated the gun turret. The young officer knew he should not have reached for the map, but thought it would only take a second. His error in judgment was the result of physical fatigue and stress during an extended training operation.

On a mountainside in Vietnam, a young private stood and raised both hands above his head, telling a helicopter pilot it was safe to lift off. Standing uphill from the helicopter, he failed to consider that the blades were much closer to the ground where he was. The soldier survived, but he lost both hands. Signaling the helicopter was not part of this soldier's responsibility. He was trying to *help* during a hasty resupply to this unit that had been operating in the jungle for more than a week.

Shortcuts are just as hazardous in the corporate environment, and great effort is required to instill discipline for safety procedures when employees are overextended, especially in manufacturing plants that are as hazardous as the weapon-filled environment of the military.

One such event occurred at a copper smelter where the furnace operator had been working double shifts for more than two months. Even though told otherwise, the furnace operator tapped the molten metal while workers climbed to the top to troubleshoot the electrodes. The sulfur-laden smoke that engulfed the workers would have been fatal had not a fast-thinking manager pulled them to safety in a control room. It took only five minutes for the furnace operator to forget his instructions and endanger many lives.

One company where I worked had a terrible safety record. Numerous lost-time accidents affected individual lives and the company's bottom line. Among the more serious accidents were two fatalities that resulted from one employee using a faulty heater to thaw a railcar discharge chute and a second who died in an explosion when he drove his forklift over a pile of hazardous material—against company safety policies. Unlike the forklift driver mentioned in Chapter 1 who recovered from a crushed pelvis, this driver died from his burns. These safety violations were fatal, regardless of the thinking behind the shortcuts. No matter whether they were the result of fatigue, inattention, stress, or simple neglect, the result was the same.

Another company where I worked had a similar set of circumstances until the CEO took action to end the accidents and injuries. To avoid accidents caused by inattention, the CEO implemented a safety education and awareness program, bringing in experts to teach the subjects and then encouraging supervisors to make constant reminders. To combat the accidents caused by fatigue, the company conducted an audit to determine the ideal number of employees per shift. Some departments lost employees; others hired additional people to provide relief for employees in tiring jobs and to avoid the persistent overtime the company experienced. Supervisors were consulted to determine which jobs needed additional vacation days to overcome both fatigue and stress.

Combining these actions with some of the other stress-relieving strategies discussed in this book, the CEO turned around an atrocious safety record and went for more than three years without a lost-time injury or accident. The additional costs for safety education and personnel were quickly recovered by a decrease in absenteeism, lowered insurance costs, and increased productivity. An investment in resilience helps make a better workplace and improve net profit.

The Role of Nutrition in Sustaining Resiliency

Even though combat situations sometimes keep soldiers from eating properly, the Army recognizes the importance of proper nutrition in combat operations. If you expect top performance, the same thing goes for corporate operations. Whether the situation is hazardous or routine, it is important to schedule and encourage adequate nutrition.

The scheduled breaks and snack room facilities are not just for the comfort of the employees involved; they are essential to both safety and resilience. In one of the companies where I worked, we found that employees produced more defect-free items per shift when we scheduled two more fifteen-minute breaks to relieve the monotony and stress of the repetitive work. Sometimes soldiers and civilians alike are too busy to eat at the scheduled times, and lowered performance can be expected when the body's fuel source is inadequate. So during those extra breaks just mentioned, free beverages and snacks were also provided, giving a little energy boost to those who didn't eat meals properly.

It is almost impossible for people to bounce back quickly when their nutrition is out of balance. If people fail to eat properly, some of life's irritants become major problems: attitudes change, people lose confidence, people break under stress, and health issues become more common. To counteract these problems during stressful times, leaders must give attention to their employees' frequency of meals, as well as each meal's amount of food and its nutritional value. I can almost hear some readers shouting at me, "They're adults. They can take care of their own food," or "How can I control what they eat? It's a free country."

I agree. You cannot control what people eat at work or off the job, but controlling people isn't always the best motivator anyway. You can influence people with seminars, training literature, personal examples, mentors, competition, corporate culture, and personal encouragement. Bringing food into the workplace at just the right time can improve morale, raise energy levels, and increase resilience—for example, pizzas for the office employees, fruit trays for customer service staff, grilled hotdogs and brats for truck drivers. There are plenty of nutritious heart-smart, cholesterol-lowering, sodium-controlled, high-protein foods as well as alternatives for vegetarians and contrarians.

Some companies have constructed on-site cafeterias where inexpensive, nutritious food encourages employees to remain at the company during meals. Employees see the cut-rate prices as a big job benefit, but the benefit to the company's bottom line is probably greater. In addition to being morale boosters, the cafeterias cut down on tardiness in returning to the job after meals, improve the chances of employees eating nutritious meals, and give the company dietitian another chance to emphasize proper eating habits.

You really shouldn't hear any complaints about the budget either. An investment in any of these programs to ensure proper nutrition can do the following:

- Provide employees good, inexpensive food
- Decrease the amount of time spent off-site for meals
- Improve eating habits with improved immune systems
- Improve absenteeism
- Lower medical costs
- Minimize insurance costs
- Lower stress
- Improve productivity
- Increase net profits
- Improve corporate resiliency

The Army gets these results by training mess sergeants to provide nutritional food and adapt meals to the unit's workload. High-energy foods are served during periods of high stress, and commanders pay special attention to the appearance and appeal of the food. Leaders frequently inspect their mess halls and eat with the troops to ensure quality and appeal.

Food is one of the stress relievers talked about in Chapter 2, and many stress experts recommend several small meals each day, rather than the traditional three square meals or the modern hit-or-miss approach. The small nutritious meals or snacks keep the energy level up and preclude the dips in blood sugar that can shorten the attention span and cause headaches, cravings, and fatigue. During scheduled training breaks, many Army commanders serve extra meals or snacks to control stress and maximize performance. Whenever possible, combat commanders bring in hot meals to help control stress and maintain resiliency among frontline soldiers.

If your company cannot implement all of these ideas, using some of them or your own creative strategies to improve nutrition can still make a difference. As military and corporate leaders have learned, the benefits of proper nutrition far outweigh the costs.

The Role of Combat Loads in Sustaining Resiliency

Combat soldiers have two basic supply loads when they confront the enemy: their combat gear (weapons, bullets, explosives, maps, night-vision devices, bulletproof vests, etc.) and their personal supplies (food, blankets, shelter, a change of socks, hygiene items, etc.). This combined load weighs probably twice the recommended weight for anyone to carry for an extended distance.

Soldiers have a way of eliminating unnecessary weight from their rucksacks. They simply get rid of every ounce of nonessential gear. While few corporate employees are confronted with such a load of equipment to carry, the concept of maintaining only essential equipment applies to the corporate workplace.

You can provide proper apparel and minimize the "combat load" for employees who have to work in stressfully hot or cold conditions or in areas where their clothing gets wet or dirty. These conditions are among the highest workplace stressors, and you can easily remove the stress by providing adequate clothing. For those employees who have to stand all day or work in hazardous areas, you can provide proper footwear to avoid injuries and reduce fatigue. You can improve morale and reduce stress and strain by throwing away those wobbly office chairs and antique desks. Your local office furniture supplier can advise you on contemporary, ergonomically designed equipment.

These items might seem luxurious, but each of these nice-to-have items has the following effects:

- Increases efficiency through improved productivity
- Improves morale by showing how much you care about employee well-being
- Decreases stress through comfort and proper physical support
- Builds resiliency by helping less-stressed employees respond better to the unexpected

Combat leaders are responsible for making sure soldiers have the necessary equipment without having them carry so much that they cannot function. Likewise, corporate leaders who want to maximize corporate resiliency make sure employees have a balanced combat load—the tools to do the job without the unnecessary stress of dated or worn-out equipment.

The Role of Physical Fitness in Sustaining Resiliency

The U.S. Army's exacting physical fitness requirements are far more than just another way to haze soldiers. They are mission essential. As explained in the Army field manual FM 6-22.5, *Combat Stress,* "Good physical conditioning delays fatigue, builds confidence, and shortens recovery times from illness and injury." It also prepares individuals to cope with the physiological demands of stress.

Many combat units start the day with organized physical training—the tougher the unit, the tougher the training. It isn't unusual to find combat units completing five-mile runs before breakfast. Other units include obstacle courses in their daily regimen. The elite troops train with full combat gear, just to make sure they are ready when called upon.

The benefits that come from physical fitness have convinced many companies to provide exercise rooms on-site and aerobic training during work hours. Others subsidize fees at health clubs or negotiate discounts for employees. Some company leaders still consider physical exercise and health club programs to be a luxury, but evidence shows that physical fitness provides many benefits to the company. The California Health Collaborative, a coalition of health promotion organizations, has assembled more than thirty studies that show that fit employees miss work less often, have fewer medical situations, avoid serious injury where fitness is a factor, and find work much less stressful.[4] All of this adds up to better lives for the employees and a better bottom line for the companies. Maximum performance of office workers might not require daily five-mile runs with a forty-pound rucksack, weapons, and combat gear, but a modest routine has proven to improve workers' efforts in the office.

The four measures used by the Army to prevent performance degradation are equally important in your company. If you want to sustain resiliency and outperform the competition, you should consider each of those measures: safety, food intake (nutrition), combat load (equipment), and physical fitness. Start with whatever you can implement immediately and build on your success.

Now that you've seen how the Army encourages resiliency, Chapter 10 illustrates the nine principles of war that guide commanders in preparing for battle.

Notes

1. Aaron Wildavsky, *Searching for Safety*, Transaction Publishing: Piscataway, NJ. June 1988.
2. Army field manual FM 6-22.5, *Combat Stress*, pp. 20–23.
3. Ibid., p. 20.
4. The California Health Collaborative, a group of California health promotion organizations, confirms these findings with more than thirty studies posted on their website ca-takeaction.com.

10

CHANNELING FEAR INTO FOCUS

★

Five weeks after the World War II landing at Normandy, Allied forces paused to strengthen their supply line with food, fuel, and ammunition. At the same time, Allied intelligence revealed that the Germans were short of supplies and troops. This information indicated that a German counterattack was unlikely so soon after they had been driven back from the coast.

With this assumption, Allied commanders established a very long line of defense with the weakest stretch through the Ardennes Forest, which spans the border region of Belgium and Luxembourg. The dense forest restricted travel for heavy tanks and trucks and, for the Germans, was the worst area for an armored counterattack if they did decide to make a move.

Germany had its own intelligence-gathering network, and based on reports about the thinly defended front in the Ardennes, Hitler went against his staff's advice and demanded a counterattack across terrain that substantially limited his tanks and wheeled vehicles. With more than 500,000 soldiers, Germany attacked the weakest point in a line of more than 650,000 American and British Allied soldiers, starting the battle that history books would call the Battle of the Bulge.

The Allies responded to the surprise attack with unexpected tenacity. Many of the troops were prepared for this type of warfare, but others were new to combat. As the Germans broke through the front lines, some of the Allied support units were still waiting for supplies and not even equipped for combat. A number of Allied units were overwhelmed and captured within hours. Others held their positions against all odds.

The resolve of these soldiers can be seen in Richard Raymond III's article "Parker's Crossroads: The Alamo Defense." He describes a critical road junction guarded by an eclectic collection of units assembled by a staff officer whose own unit was decimated. Fewer than three hundred men defended the narrow passage against a German panzer division for two days. When the small unit finally collapsed, some of the men escaped through the forest to join other outfits, but their bravery in delaying the enemy gave the Allied command time to respond to the German's gigantic counterattack.[1] The battle across the entire front lasted a little more than six weeks, killing 19,000 Americans and approximately 100,000 Germans. Another 200,000 Allies and Germans were wounded or captured.

The kind of heroism demonstrated at the crossroads and at dozens of similar points across the Ardennes resulted from resilient leadership and great moral resolve. Units with less fortitude could not have held up against these panzer divisions. The keys to military victory in desperate times such as the Battle of the Bulge are control of combat forces and a clear vision for what must be done. The fear normally associated with combat and its accompanying stress can help soldiers perform well while its leadership embraces a well-tested doctrine of warfare. The U.S. Army's doctrine for such times is spelled out in the *Principles of War*, first printed in a 1921 training regulation. While these principles have been adjusted over time, they are still the bedrock of Army doctrine in times of war and are a part of the Army field manual FM 100-5, *Operations*.[2]

Working through these nine principles of war, you will see how the Army uses them to reduce stress and remain focused in times of

U.S. Army's Principles of War

1. Objective
2. Offensive
3. Mass
4. Economy of force
5. Maneuver
6. Unity of command
7. Security
8. Surprise
9. Simplicity

combat. You'll also see how they are just as applicable in business as they are in combat.

Objective

Army field manual FM 100-5, *Operations*, describes warfare's ultimate objective as the destruction of the enemy and its will to fight. To achieve this end, Army commanders designate physical objectives, such as key cities, hilltops, road junctions, or other essential targets, and the operations at all levels are coordinated to reach these physical objectives.

Vague, uncertain, unstated, or unwritten objectives make it impossible for either military or corporate business units to reach their goals.

> "Direct every military operation toward a clearly defined, decisive, and attainable objective."
>
> **—Army field manual FM 100-5, *Operations***

Clearly stated objectives are essential for minimizing stress and overall success. As with the Army's objectives, your own goals need to be the following:

- Positive, precise, and specific as to what you will accomplish
- Measurable so you will know when the goal is accomplished
- Challenging enough to be worthwhile but also realistic and achievable
- Set within a specific period to keep you on track

Once you have established what you want to do, you can apply the remaining principles of war to your business situation.

Offensive

Taking the offensive is so essential to controlling the battlefield that the Army maintains an offensive spirit even when they must temporarily take up a defensive posture. In the Battle of the Bulge, the Allies were forced into a defensive posture to reestablish their supply line, but only those forces immediately facing the Germans were in a static defense. Units not directly engaged were sent around the flanks of the German panzer divisions to attack them from the sides and rear.

The same principle applies in the corporate arena. If your company is always on the defensive, you can only react to the competition. You have to respond to the competition's price reductions, product introductions, innovative distributions, personnel benefit programs, creative marketing, and so on. Stress runs high when you are the one who always responds, because continuously being on the defensive is difficult and demoralizing. Being on the offensive means being in attack mode.

> "Offensive: Seize, retain, and exploit the initiative."
>
> **—Army field manual FM 100-5, *Operations***

If your company is on the defensive, you can find ways to turn things around by consulting with your business advisers, board of directors, team members, mastermind groups, industry consultants, academic advisers, or government resources. A review of the basic management tools also sometimes provides overlooked solutions. Advisers, consultants, and team members might show you strategies that can put you on the offensive and make the competition react to your moves.

In addition to seizing and retaining the offensive, this principle of war includes the concept of exploiting the initiative. If the competition shows any sign of weakness when you go on the offensive, you need to continue in your efforts. You must not stop when you reach your first goal; rather, you must use this success to leverage even greater success toward your ultimate objective. Corporations must exploit the initiative to maximize the value of their investments. There is little glory in bringing a "me too" product to market and watching it share shelf space with the competition. If you have a winner, take all the market share you can get. The following principles of war will help you understand how to do this.

Mass

In the first Gulf War, Saddam Hussein and his advisers knew that a coalition amphibious landing might be a feint, but U.S. Navy and Marine units conducted practice exercises in the waters off Iraq and the media reported every action. Iraq had to establish a defense against this possibility.

> "Mass the effects of overwhelming combat power at the decisive place and time."
>
> **—Army field manual FM 100-5, *Operations***

One hundred percent of the remaining coalition assets were focused on Iraq's critical frontline positions or assets far to the rear of the battle line. This concentration of resources, based on the principle of mass, overwhelmed the Iraqis and brought a quick end to their fighting ability. The same principle was applied in 2003, and the Iraqis could not resist physically or psychologically.

Massing combat power applies just as well to corporate operations. Companies that focus their resources on specific objectives are much more successful than fragmented businesses. When opening new stores, for example, Wal-Mart supplies all the required resources to make sure the store succeeds. Good benefits attract good employees, corporate specialists provide the training, and focused advertising brings in the customers. Wal-Mart does not sneak up on a community. They mass their forces and strive for success.

Fragmented teams can be reorganized to gain focus. The textile company where I worked had three divisions, and each served different parts of the market. The finishing division prepared fabric for use in the clothing and furniture industry; the converting division served the furniture and bedding manufacturing markets, and the drapery division sold to the home furnishings market. We were a tough competitor when corporate leaders massed the forces of two or more of these divisions to reduce the prices of finished products or to position inventory to serve customers.

> "Massing effects enables numerically inferior forces to achieve decisive results while limiting exposure to enemy fire."
>
> **—Army field manual 100-5,** *Operations*

You can mass your forces in a similar way by collaborating with other divisions in your company or by developing alliances with others who serve the same customers. Procedures can be developed to include all of your company's resources to apply maximum combat power to the situation. Being on the offensive requires constant learning and frequent contact with customers, but the offensive action results in positive stress instead of the negative reactions from being on the defense.

Economy of Force

When commanders go to war they use all of their combat power, but they make sure it is used in the most effective way possible. Sometimes, the most effective way to beat the enemy is to attack with everything you have, straight ahead. At other times, commanders use some of their force to deceive the enemy into thinking the attack is coming from another direction. If the deception works, fewer enemy soldiers are available for guarding the main approach, such as in General Schwartzkopf's use of the Navy and Marines to deceive Iraqi commanders in the Gulf War.

> "Employ all combat power available in the most effective way possible; allocate minimum essential combat power to secondary efforts."
>
> **—Army field manual FM 100-5, *Operations***

You must make these kinds of decisions about the most effective use of your resources. Sometimes you might want to distract the competition by making overtures to customers you don't really intend to pursue. At other times, you will want to dedicate all of your resources to a single, focused objective, avoiding any kind of distraction. If your company is focused on gaining market share and filling manufacturing capacity, every component in your company should be involved in some way. Don't be distracted by new product opportunities, mergers, acquisitions, or anything else that seems like a good deal—unless these activities help you reach your objective.

As much as any of the other principles of war, economy of force provides clarity and focus and makes sure everything you do is essential to your mission.

Maneuver

The principle of maneuver is taught to brand-new second lieutenants as they train for combat. They learn to limit the enemy's maneuver with a base of fire while part of their platoon moves forward or circles to attack from a different vantage point.

Combat units need to be flexible in the midst of battle, adapting to circumstances as they happen, and higher commanders with the bigger picture must continuously direct the efforts of combat units. While Allied troops held the Germans at the Ardennes Forest crossroads, Allied commanders sent General George Patton's tank-heavy army to attack around the left end of the German's line of defense and cut off their supplies, reinforcements, and maneuver capability. Instead of simply shooting back at the attacking enemy, Allied commanders placed their own units on the offensive, cutting off the Germans' supplies and reducing Germany's ability to respond to other actions across the front.

> "Place the enemy in a position of disadvantage through the flexible application of combat power."
>
> **—Army field manual FM 100-5, *Operations***

Corporate leaders can use the principle of maneuver by shifting to meet the efforts of competitors. At one point, they might want to defend against a price increase, and at another time they might want to attack the competition's other products. Sometimes, revenue might be spent on additional sales staff, but if that isn't working, the money might be used to bring in additional advertising staff.

Early in my corporate career, I learned the value of attacking when the competition was vulnerable. When a major competitor ventured out of his home territory to offer deep discounts to our major customers, we had to act fast to hold onto market share. Since the competitor didn't lower prices to his own customers, a head-to-head fight would have been a no-win proposition. We would have lost money if we lowered our price to all of these customers, even if we picked up some of his market share in the process. Bringing the price back up after the battle would have taken years.

> "Maneuver is dynamic warfare that rejects predictable patterns of operations."
>
> **—Army field manual FM 100-5, *Operations***

We knocked the competitor off balance, however, by acquiring special inventory of a different product—one that was part of his base load. We used our sister division's warehouse in his territory and sold products to his primary customers at break-even pricing, pretty much as he had done to our own customers. We did not make any money with the maneuver, but it cost us very little, and we kept our market share at reasonable prices. The aggressive maneuvering caused the competitor to withdraw his small-margin offers and pay attention to his own profitable business instead of playing around in our territory.

The next time a competitor goes after your customers with a price or product, attack the scoundrel where he least expects it. As a defensive maneuver, you can make contingency plans for these situations. You know the attack is coming, so get ready for it. Just as important, if you plan to attack your competitors, be aware that they, too, will be maneuvering. Guard your flanks.

The principle of maneuver is critical in controlling both military and corporate combat, and your teams will maintain their confidence knowing that you can hold your own against competitors, you still have the customer base, and their jobs are secure.

Unity of Command

When the United States goes to war, all services involved should report to a single commander who establishes objectives, makes sure units can communicate, employs the principles of war, and makes the ultimate decisions of who will do what. This single command structure is known by the military as *unity of command*.

> "For every objective, seek unity of command and unity of effort."
>
> **—Army field manual FM 100-5, *Operations***

One would think that American forces have always used this commonsense approach, especially since our media reports everything they can about the military. Complications still exist, however. For example, when the U.S. Army deployed to Somalia in 1993, the humanitarian aid effort turned to disaster and eighteen soldiers were killed.

The key factor in this failure was a violation of the unity of command principle. Three forces conducted operations under three separate commands. The chain of command was vague, the objectives mixed, and the equipment and units unable to communicate properly. C. Kenneth Allard, author and analyst for the U.S. Department of Defense, quoted the infamous Murphy's law of armed combat, saying, "If it takes more than ten seconds to explain command arrangements, they probably won't work."[3] In Somalia, the Army was reminded that unity of command is just as important in noncombat operations as it is in battle.

Until recent years, most American companies understood the principle of unity of command. The pyramid structure seen on traditional organizational charts shows the boss at the top, middle managers on the second line, and frontline managers working directly with the majority of the employees. This traditional arrangement is known as a vertical management structure, and the person whose name occupies the top box on the organizational chart is, unquestionably, the person with authority to commit resources, make decisions about the operation, and direct who does what.

An alternative arrangement, the functional management structure, has people reporting to different managers for different purposes. Just looking at the solid lines and dotted lines crisscrossing the organizational chart can give you a headache. The uncertainty of dual reporting creates a lot of stress for line managers who receive conflicting orders from production managers and quality supervisors. There is much less stress, however, if you know who the boss is.

If you have partnered with a sister division to support a customer, you know how important it is to decide who will be the *supreme* commander because divisions can sometimes disagree about who should do what. Getting a decision about who is in charge should be done before a conflict arises. You won't be sorry you spent time establishing a command structure where the chain of command is easily identifiable and easy to follow.

Security

Army leaders are responsible for the security of their people. This means protecting them from the enemy and from themselves—accidents can be just as disastrous as armed conflict. Commanders must set up security measures that will keep people safe and available for duty.

In the same way, corporate leaders must also provide security for their employees and organizations by taking precautions against threats such as safety hazards, competitive forces, changing markets, and other volatile situations. Employees feel better about their workplace, and stress is reduced, when they can see management utilizing security measures such as the following:

> "Never let the enemy acquire unfair advantage."
>
> **—Army field manual FM 100-5, *Operations***

- Restrict work areas such as accounting, computer technology, and corporate offices that need to be secured to prevent misuse of personnel data, financial records, and customer records.
- Information security is important, such as carefully processing all customer, employee, and corporate records and shredding them when unneeded, both drafts and final documents.
- Financial security almost goes without saying, but special procedures need to be established and reviewed to ensure proper handling of cash and other receivables to protect the assets and the reputation of those responsible for the procedures.

> "Knowledge and understanding of enemy strategy, tactics, and doctrine are important in developing adequate security measures."
>
> **—Army field manual FM 100-5, *Operations***

- Guards are important to control access to the workplace, property, and parking lots.
- Fences help provide security around the entire perimeter of workplace and interior open spaces.

- Lighting is critical for safety and security inside the workplace and in parking areas.
- Emergency evacuation plans, education, and practices are a major component of all security programs.
- Emergency alarms are an integral component of security, and you have to make sure they are tested and working on a regular schedule.
- Fire protection can be implemented with sprinkler systems, automatic reporting, fire alarms, and practice.
- OSHA safety precautions are for the benefit of employees and the company, so someone has to be responsible for proper safety training, equipment safety guards, and enforced lockouts.
- Seminars conducted by supervisors or outside training consultants are the basis for a good training program. Any money invested in safety is easily recouped in savings of time, injuries, insurance, and liability claims.

Less visible to most employees but just as important are security measures that help run the business well:

- Security alarms protect sensitive work areas and provide personal safety around dangerous equipment or work areas.
- Audits of corporate policies and performance provide added security for employees and financial, safety, and health data.
- Competitive threats can be discovered through careful analysis of new or changing situations in the industries you serve.
- Market threats can undermine your security without your proper analysis of changes that will affect corporate profits and employee jobs.
- Technology can be a part of your security program, or it can be a threat. A routine and continuing analysis of techno-logical changes can enhance your company's position and save jobs.

- Training and education are important to the security of your company as you prepare management, both senior and junior, and employees to stay ahead of the competition and market forces.

Everyone feels better when they understand the security measures taken to protect them and the company. You can control stress, increase performance, and increase productivity by communicating all the security plans your company develops, procedures implemented, and money invested to provide additional security. Your employees don't expect to know all the details, rather just enough to assure them of their job security.

Surprise

Surprising the enemy is a good thing. If you catch them off balance, the surprise can shift the balance of power or it can ensure victory with minimum effort and loss of life. Catching the enemy off guard prevents their best response and gives you a psychological edge for success. The *effect* is what you're after with this principle. Total surprise isn't always possible nor is it always required, because enemies who know of your impending attack might not have time to do anything about it.

> "Strike the enemy at a time or place or in a manner for which he is unprepared."
>
> **—Army field manual FM 100-5, *Operations***

The Army's field manual FM 100-5, *Operations*, explains that the following factors contribute to surprise:

- **Speed**—overwhelming speed of approach
- **Intelligence**—knowing information the enemy thinks secret
- **Deception**—feints, maneuvers, disinformation, intentions
- **Combat power**—application of unexpected power, number of troops, or violent attack

- Security—operational security
- **Variations**—of tactics, combat methods, size of force, direction of attack, location of main effort, and timing

The problem with surprise is that it works both ways. Pearl Harbor was an unparalleled success for the Japanese, though it brought them to a tragic end years later. The Al-Qaeda attack on the Pentagon and World Trade Center is a more recent example of the effectiveness of surprise combat actions. While U.S. intelligence agencies knew of this possible threat for years, the attackers accomplished their mission by varying earlier tactics and combat methods.

> "The enemy need not be taken completely by surprise but only become aware too late to react effectively."
>
> **—Army field manual FM 100-5, *Operations***

Businesses can also use surprise to gain advantage, but just as with the military, they can be surprised themselves, too. The corporate surprises that make the news are usually the opposite of what the involved corporations want. These include unreported losses, mergers (surprise to employees), surprise quarterly losses, legislative surprises, surprise slumps, downturn in business, surprise departures, and surprise retirements. To avoid surprises like these, you must pay attention to the principles of security.

On the other hand, if you plan surprises against your competition, you gain control in the marketplace and have freedom to execute plans to your advantage. Remember the Army's purpose in using surprise—to shift the balance of power and succeed with minimum effort. The elements of surprise are discussed in more detail in Chapter 13.

Simplicity

One of the first acronyms burned into the minds of young sergeants and officers is *KISS*, "Keep it simple, stupid." Every plan developed by these young leaders is influenced by a history based on simplicity. From the earliest days of American military conflict, commanders have found that simplicity works best in instruction, planning, equipment, and war fighting. Corporations have succeeded with the same kind of thinking. Lessons that are stated simply and clearly are easier to understand. The more critical the task and the greater the stress, the more likely it is that orders will be misunderstood or misremembered.

> "Prepare clear, uncomplicated plans and concise orders to ensure thorough understanding."
>
> **—Army field manual FM 100-5, *Operations***

When I went after the competitor who came into our territory to steal some of our most profitable business, I used a very simple strategy. I put inventory into a sister division's warehouse and offered it at low prices to the other guy's customers. Anything more would have complicated the effort.

Let the Principles of War Work for You

The Army emphasizes these nine principles of war because experience has shown them to be invaluable in battle. Expertise in each area increases a commander's chances of victory. You can benefit just as well in your business if you look at these principles as a way of doing business. You will not have to implement all of them at once, but you will want to review these principles with others in your company to determine what you are already doing well and where improvements can be made.

Once you have clear and concise business objectives, you can work your way through the rest of the principles to make sure your company is on the offensive and that you are properly using the other seven principles to take advantage of the competition—mass, economy of force, maneuver, unity of command, security, surprise, and simplicity.

If you do these things, you will control stress and channel fear into focus. You will have a definite advantage in the marketplace, because many companies are still using a haphazard, unfocused approach to corporate battle. Now that you understand the principles that guide the Army in combat, Chapter 11 shows the effectiveness of Army planning and what it can do for your company.

Notes

1. Richard Raymond III, sergeant first class (Ret.), "Parker's Crossroads: The Alamo Defense," *The Cub Magazine*, 106th Infantry Division Association, 1993.
2. Army field manual FM 100-5, Operations, Headquarters, U.S. Army, Washington, D.C., 1993.
3. C. Kenneth Allard, *Lessons Learned: Somalia and Joint Doctrine*, Defense Technical Information Center, Department of Defense, Autumn 1995.

11

YOUR BATTLE PLAN

★

The U.S. Army considers every detail in planning operations and disseminates information to each level of leadership with a five-paragraph field order that is just as standard as the nine principles of war discussed in the previous chapter.

As outlined in the following sidebar, the field order is always presented in the same numerical sequence, with the first paragraph describing the enemy and friendly situations and the second paragraph stating the mission, or the objective. The details of the third, fourth, and fifth paragraphs vary, depending on the type of unit. For example, a six-man reconnaissance patrol requires different information than do combat engineer companies preparing to bridge a major river.

However, all units use the same five major categories of information, and commanders at all levels recognize a five-paragraph field order by its headings and format. Every major staff member provides input, and the outline acts as a template for developing the overall plan, ensuring that coordination and planning are complete.

Planning Tools in Business

In some respects, the five-paragraph field order is similar to corporate planning documents such as business plans, business opera-

Five-Paragraph Field Order

1. **Situation:** enemy and friendly
2. **Mission:** the objective; what is to be achieved
3. **Execution:** the concept of the operation, mission of subordinate units, and coordinating instructions
4. **Service support:** food, ammunition, uniform and equipment requirements, and handling of wounded soldiers and captured personnel and equipment
5. **Command and signal:** chain of command and details of communication signals (radio and visual)

tions plans, and project management schedules. The main difference between the field order and these corporate documents is in their scope. Business plans are typically used as a point of reference until something requires an update, such as a description of the company and products, customer benefits, analysis of the market, strategies, financial arrangements, and the management team. Business operations plans typically describe the type of business being considered as well as the location, the type of facilities involved, purchasing and sales procedures, quality control, and so on. Project management plans are related to the five-paragraph field order in that both documents are used to guide operations, ensuring complete coordination and communications.

How to Get All the Information

Making detailed plans requires a depth of knowledge about your company, suppliers, customers, competitors, and the marketplace. In one of my previous companies, we learned all we could about our own products and those we used in manufacturing. Downstream, we visited our customer's suppliers as well as the customers of our customers. We researched the organizations and industries we could not visit. The more we understood about our customer's marketplace, the better we could serve the people who counted on us.

Upstream, we researched and visited our own suppliers and the companies that supplied their needs. Everyone was surprised when we visited some of our own competitors. All we had to do was ask!

The more we learned about each industry, the better we understood the impact and implications of changes in the economy, markets, labor force, weather, and social conditions. The more knowledgeable we became, the more confident and stress free we were about the many factors that influenced the sale and use of our products.

One of our own senior managers misunderstood our pursuit of industry knowledge and declared that we were wasting our time. "Sales professionals don't need this type of information," he insisted. "All they have to know is our own products." This vice president was often surprised by swings in the marketplace, because he failed to understand the importance of detailed planning, the psychology of selling, and stress control. This informational recluse understood the impact of market forces only when they were analyzed by trade journals and the evening news. Instead of understanding what was going on and predicting changes before they occurred, he reacted to events after they happened. Not only was he more stressed than necessary, but his incomplete knowledge caused him to give stress to everyone else in his sphere of influence.

In another situation, I had the wonderful experience of serving two of America's most sophisticated companies, Alcoa and U.S. Steel. Both companies are globally oriented and professionally trained to gather information that could influence their production and sales. Because these companies analyze every aspect of the market, they are seldom surprised by events that influence their market. They don't always preempt situations, but they are way ahead of competitors in finding solutions to the problems. Likewise, these company leaders are seldom stressed by changes that affect their companies, suppliers, or customers. Improved communications of their plans is a key factor in improving routine performance or meeting the inevitable crises.

How to Be Better Informed

In this age of informational overload, it seems odd that people don't know some of the most basic details that influence their work. With information at the touch of the fingers, people seem unable to access critical pieces of the puzzle. Cell phones and palm displays carry the news of the world, yet people don't know what tomorrow's schedule holds for them.

In the old days, corporate managers spent hours picking the brains of contemporaries, subordinates, and competitors. While others interpreted the facts and passed along their opinions, corporate leaders formulated their own understanding and developed strategies to act and react.

As the corporate management structure became flatter and flatter, managers at all levels were swept aside, and employees were expected to do more, be more, and decide more—all for the same pay, of course. Contemporary managers' schedules were stretched to the point of breaking because these managers had more and more people reporting to them. Accurate and complete communications became rarer and rarer because the leaders just didn't have time to manage and communicate as they should.

On the other hand, the traditional vertical management structure ensures that each leader guides the efforts of only a few subordinate managers. Line managers have only a small number of people reporting directly to them. Everyone up and down the chain of command is assured of accurate and complete information for operations and reporting.

Newsletters and e-mails cannot replace the solid guidance of experienced managers who have a good handle on the information flow. While both have an important place in the corporate environment, face-to-face interaction between people is different from remote high-tech communication. The technical relay of communication is better than no communication at all, but the presence of live managers does wonders for improving information flow, reducing stress, and increasing productivity.

Corporate Use of the Five-Paragraph Operation Order

Companies can adapt the Army's five-paragraph field order in their own planning initiatives by including as many of its elements as possible in routine communications. Sound management of individuals and departments leads to a clearer understanding of what needs to be done, and clearer understanding reduces negative stress.

Leaders at all levels have opportunities to implement a process comparable to the Army's five-paragraph field order. Whether in manufacturing, sales, customer service, or any of the other areas, managers can use a structured document to assign specific missions and objectives. Companies who choose to increase market share will find the military template useful in assembling all pertinent information and ensuring complete support throughout the organization. A five-paragraph field order will pull together the company's resources in support of the sales objectives. The sales team can confront the competition knowing that the entire team is supporting them with marketing, advertising, customer service, product management, manufacturing, distribution, accounting, and technical support. Every manager in the company can be informed of the mission's objectives, its importance to the company, and how they fit into the larger operation.

To use the Army's five-paragraph field order, start by filling out the following template. Modify it to suit your own businesses.

1. **Situation:** competitive and friendly

   a. Information about competitive situations

      - What is the competitive posture concerning this area of interest?
      - What are their strengths and weaknesses?
      - What seasonal influences affect this operation?
      - What is the competitive activity nationally and internationally? And in each region?
      - How well do competitors meet industry standards?
      - What is the market share of each competitor?
      - How important is this market to the competitor? How will they react?
      - What advantage does the competition find in their operating methods?
      - Are there entry barriers to preclude additional competitors?
      - Does the competition have any other advantages that will affect this mission?
      - What are the trends in the industry?

- How are competitors influenced by legal and environmental factors?
- What is known about the competition from research directly from the competition, customers, suppliers, media, forecasters, associations, employees, and so on?

b. Information about friendly situations

- Why are we considering making changes?
- What is the mission of the other departments, divisions, or next higher organization with regard to this subject?
- What are our strengths and weaknesses?
- What are current costs associated with this process?
- What are the forecasted costs?
- What are the forecasted consequences of the status quo?
- What trends can we see internally?
- What support is available to help accomplish the mission?
- Do we have any corporate advantages that will impact this mission?

c. Attachments and detachments (i.e., what kind of outside support will you receive or what must you give up to support another manager?)

- Will special, temporary, or permanent support staff be assigned to the departments during this operation?
- Will any staff be detached or reassigned during this operation?
- Are consultants available?
- Do we have any special advisers to achieve the mission?

d. List of outside influences with details (weather, seasonal business, national economy, monetary conversion rates, strength of the manufacturing sector, information sector, medical influences, technology, agriculture, etc.)

2. **Mission:** Clearly state in one sentence what must be accomplished. Examples:

- Manufacturing will reduce inventory costs by 3 percent within the next ninety days.
- Sales will increase sales revenue by 5 percent within the next six months.
- We will achieve 20 percent production increase by July 15.
- Accounting will reduce aged receivables by 7 percent within the next forty-five days.
- Customer service will establish a system of tracking customer complaints by the end of the month.

3. **Execution**
   a. Concept of operation: establish the overall plan for completing the mission.

   b. Mission of subordinate and supporting units: list the specific mission of others in support of the department's primary mission, including any special support, equipment, or personnel they will receive.

   c. Coordinating instructions: in this paragraph, combat units include information such as the following:

      - Time of departure and return
      - Formations and order of movement
      - Route of travel
      - Passage of friendly positions
      - Rally points
      - Actions at the objective
      - Rehearsals
      - After-action reviews (AARs)

Some of these items are unnecessary for corporate plans, but businesses need similar coordinating instructions. The corporate template includes coordinating instructions that will help accomplish the business mission:

- Travel instructions, if required
- Liaison with other organizations

- Target dates and schedules for submitting progress reports
- Type of progress report expected
- Rehearsals and/or practice schedules if appropriate
- AARs

4. **Service support:** the corporate model can modify the military's concern with food, ammunition, and handling of prisoners of war by including the following instead:

   - What support will corporate headquarters and other divisions provide?
   - How will other departments support the mission efforts?
   - Will other departments concede part of their expense budget to help reach this objective?
   - Will vendors or suppliers provide special assistance?
   - What special equipment will be provided?

5. **Command and communications:** the established chain of command will probably be followed, but special authority might be delegated to specific managers during the operation. Make a list of the following:

   - Special communications tools that will be provided
   - Unique levels of authority to communicate outside the chain of command or other departments
   - Expectations for high-tech or face-to-face communications
   - Procedures for communicating any unexpected or bad news (The stressfulness of bad news is minimized if operations orders include specific methods on how to communicate this news. Leaders should make it clear that they welcome news that is unfavorable for the operation.)
   - Public relations, media announcements, spokespersons, and other communications (These can be included to complement or support the designated mission.)

- Expected methods and frequency of communications:
  (1) personal briefings, (2) internal and external
  newsletters, (3) memos and letters, (4) technology—
  e-mail, voice mail, palm devices, cell phone
- Methods of message distribution

Complete five-paragraph field orders typically have a number of
attachments to provide all the details needed by commanders. In the
military, information included in the attachments are details such as
maps and overlays; radio frequencies and call signs; high-tech support; engineering plans for construction of roads, bridges, obstacles,
and buildings; artillery and air support; intelligence analysis, reconnaissance, surveillance, and so on.

Business attachments should include things such as maps and overlays showing the location of facilities or areas of responsibilities,
communications equipment and procedures to be used, authoriza-
tion to leapfrog the chain of command if appropriate, departmental
plans in support of the objective, and intelligence analysis. The purpose of the attachment is to display the details that are too cumbersome for the actual field order. All pertinent information is
suitable for attachments.

The Details Are Critical

The Army places high priority on the planning process and evaluates
the ability of combat units during annual training tests such as the
brigade-level tests conducted at the U.S. Army's National Training
Center in California. The evaluations are objective and some of the
information is available to the public. As can be seen in Tables 11-1
and 11-2, the Army is amazingly candid in displaying these results as
reported by the Center for Army Lessons Learned.[1]

A quick scan of Tables 11-1 and 11-2 illustrates the kinds of problems associated with reconnaissance and surveillance (R&S) and
shows the importance of detailed planning in a combat environment.
Officers at the brigade level have a lot of experience, but the results
show a gap in the training process. Many of the evaluated officers

Table 11-1 Planning Problems Observed During Brigade Training Tests

Inadequate Planning*

- Little command or staff involvement in planning
- Limited mainly to the "R&S Matrix" in the Intelligence Annex of the Operations Order, which provides subordinate units with only named areas of interest and perhaps observation post locations
- No clear overall objective or intent
- No adequate integration of available assets (such as overhead photos, electronic warfare efforts, or combat unit operations during the main battle)
- No deconfliction of terrain (for preventing collisions, friendly fire prevention, fratricide, etc.)
- No coordinated plans developed for insertion or extraction of assets into or out of enemy positions (some penetration of the enemy is almost always required for the gathering of information)
- No fire support plans included
- No provision for combat support or combat service support
- No plans for casualty evacuation
- No involvement of signal officers in R&S planning
- No unit standard operating procedures developed for these tasks!

Results**

- Clearance of fires extremely difficult.
- Risk of fratricide greatly increased.
- Many different elements from different units operating in the same area with no single agency knowing where everyone is
- Required coordination for passage of lines rarely affected
- Casualties incurred during reconnaissance suffer a 70–100 percent died-of-wounds rate

Summary of results: The operation lacked unity of command where a single agency knew the location of elements from different units, making the coordination of fires extremely difficult and increasing the chances of fratricide. Umpires declared that 70 to 100 percent of R&S soldiers "died of wounds" because of inadequate planning.

---

*Problems created by poor planning at brigade-level annual training test.
**Poor planning by Brigade Staff resulted in poor performance and serious operational problems.

needed to rework training plans for both planning and execution of R&S. The quote used as a caption for Table 11-1 is especially sobering when you consider that these combat-ready units are among the United States' best. However, it is rewarding to know that testing personnel had the courage to candidly note their observations and report them to the Army's highest commands.

In addition to the planning errors, the AARs include performance problems associated with these poorly planned operations orders. Table 11-2 lists these observations and results. The poor results reflect the importance of proper planning for R&S operations.

Looking at this example, one might worry about the Army's ability to plan. Keep in mind, however, that this was a test situation designed to identify weak areas. All of the soldiers involved learned from their mistakes and improved their planning and performance. Other commanders learned from the AARs and corrections were made throughout the Army. Just as in the corporate arena, it is better to identify problems in a controlled situation than during actual operations.

The Army was surprised to find the gap in their training and planning procedures for R&S. The importance of proper planning and use of detailed information is critical whether in the military or in business, because high-quality performance is nearly impossible without high-quality planning.

Table 11-2 Performance Problems Associated With Poor Planning

Performance Problems

- Units tasked to accomplish R&S missions receive very little planning time and usually inadequate guidance.
- Scout platoon leaders often get a list of Named Areas of Interest (what they are looking for) and instructions to move out in an hour.
- Junior leaders often cannot develop their own adequate control measures nor promulgate those devised by higher command echelons.

Results

- There is general confusion and lack of control.
- Units do not accomplish proper troop-leading procedures.
- Soldiers often cross the line of departure often without the proper equipment and supplies.
- Situational awareness is usually poor to nonexistent. Reconnaissance units have great difficulty recognizing fleeting tactical opportunities.
- Lack of preparation time prevents the accomplishment of required coordination with adjacent or forward units. Many scouts are killed by friendly forces as they attempt to transit the friendly security area.
- Scouts do not understand the enemy situation, leading to inappropriate movement techniques and poor decisions.
- There is a lack of flexibility. Without sufficient control measures, redirecting elements is extremely difficult when changes to the plan are required.

Inadequate planning and preparation gives the reconnaissance forces "very low probability for success." Commanders are then left without first-hand intelligence of the enemy situation, decreasing chances for success in the battle. Success of the mission and hundreds of lives are at risk because of errors in planning.

Poor planning at brigade-level resulted in poor performance at platoon level.

Planning Your Work and Working Your Plan

During a visit to a major FedEx airport hub operation, I was impressed with the calm execution of their *battle plan* in the face of an impending thunderstorm. At ten-minute intervals, the FedEx meteorological team gave updates on the exact arrival time of the storm front. The operations manager calmly gave his team leaders a *warning order* to anticipate securing aircraft, ground vehicles, and personnel when the bad weather overtook them.

Every member of the team knew their responsibilities at designated times prior to the storm's arrival. Not a minute of processing time was lost as airplane doors were closed, wheels were chocked, carts secured inside buildings, and personnel moved to designated areas inside buildings. When the storm passed, the team picked up the pace and completed their work on schedule.

When I complimented the manager on his team's performance in maximizing their use of time to keep deliveries on schedule, he explained that everyone performed well without stress because "we plan our work and work our plan." In spite of ever-changing variables, his team calmly gets the job done because they have contingency plans.

The same thinking goes for your work in the marketplace. Customer demands and competitive maneuvering can be overwhelming without some way to capture all the variables, strengths, and weaknesses that you have to deal with. Simply remembering everything that you need to tell subordinates can be overwhelming. The five-paragraph model gives you a template for keeping track of all the issues, ensuring complete coverage of the information regardless of how stressful the circumstances.

Using a template similar to the five-paragraph field order can influence corporate goal setting, mission accomplishment, and stress levels. Sometimes this model increases productivity by increasing stress and holding people accountable. It certainly helps control negative stress through improved communications and the assurance that comes with using a template as a reminder of critical details.

As a brand-new second lieutenant, I was pretty nervous in my first encounter with the five-paragraph order. The amount of information was overwhelming. But even though my head was spinning, I found comfort in the structure of the briefing and the fact that my platoon sergeant said he understood everything we were supposed to do.

The process doesn't have to be overwhelming for young managers or the leaders who use the standard five-paragraph format. Line managers and those affected by the mission assignment can provide input for the order. Corporate staff can do a lot of the initial research, and inclusion of the responsible managers ensures that they buy into the mission.

High performance takes dedication and high energy. In Chapter 12, you'll see how the Army trains for the physical stress involved in accomplishing their objectives.

Notes

1. "Reconnaissance and the Maneuver Brigade," *Combat Training Center Quarterly Bulletin*, Center for Army Lessons Learned, Fort Leavenworth, KS, September 1997.

12

DISCIPLINE

★

"Victory in war does not depend entirely upon numbers or mere courage; only skill and discipline will ensure it."

—FLAVIUS VEGETIUS RENATUS, ROMAN MILITARY ANALYST, APPROXIMATELY A.D. 375

These are the opening words to Flavius Vegetius Renatus's "The Roman Discipline the Cause of Their Greatness."[1] This epic treatise is still a part of the essential literature for military professionals, and its three sections describe training new recruits, military organization, and the strength of military units. After researching and analyzing the great armies of ancient times, many of them conquered by the Romans, Flavius Vegetius Renatus concluded that discipline is of utmost importance in winning battles. He describes in detail the training for formations, weapons, physical conditioning, and hardening of soldiers, all of which instilled the discipline he found lacking in the Roman army of his time.

Modern armies around the world use the same methods for instilling discipline. From their first day on the job, soldiers learn to stand in formation, move about as a group, and stay in step. Physical training begins immediately with daily runs and conditioning exercises. Today's weapons are more sophisticated, but the training is just as rigorous as in Roman times, and a strict regimen is in place to harden twenty-first-century warriors.

The Decline of the Great Armies

Flavius concluded that long periods of peace caused the formidable nations of old to relax their military fervor in favor of civil pursuits "and a love of idleness and ease. Hence, a relaxation of military discipline insensibly ensued, then a neglect of it, and it sunk at last into entire oblivion. The necessity, therefore, of discipline cannot be too often inculcated, as well as the strict attention requisite in the choice and training of new levies (recruits)."

Discipline Defined

The word *discipline* serves as either a noun or a verb. As a noun, *The American Heritage Dictionary* defines the word in six categories of usage.

1. training expected to produce a specific character or pattern of behavior, especially training that produces moral or mental improvement
2. controlled behavior resulting from disciplinary training; self-control
3. a. control obtained by enforcing compliance or order. b. A systematic method to obtain obedience: a military discipline. c. A state of order based on submission to rules and authority: a teacher who demanded discipline in the classroom
4. punishment intended to correct or train
5. a set of rules or methods, as those regulating the practice of a church or monastic order
6. a branch of knowledge or teaching

It seems unique that the same word defines all aspects of behavior training: the training itself, the performance of these tasks, the tasks themselves, and the punishment for behavior contrary to the training.

Users of the English language have to hear the word used in context to understand the intended definition, and it is this peculiarity that causes some misunderstanding among those unfamiliar with the Army's use of the word *discipline*. Sometimes people think that Army discipline refers only to strict rules and punishment. This is true in the sense that the Army has an extensive system of rules and an entire branch of the Army dedicated to administering these rules.

Military punishment, however, results when there is a breakdown in the discipline that old Flavius considered so important. If individual and unit discipline were sufficient, there would be no violations requiring judicial punishment. If the discipline of self-control and orderly performance were sufficient, the Army could complete its missions and achieve victory on the battlefield. Breaches of good order and discipline weaken the Army in peacetime and in combat. Lack of self-discipline creates undesirable situations for everyone, whether civilian or military.

Well-disciplined Army units perform well in the face of danger. Chapter 1 referred to the increased battle fatigue and negative stress reactions that result from poor discipline. Likewise, well-disciplined individuals are more likely to experience positive stress than are the poorly disciplined individuals, who instead experience negative stress reactions. Flavius Vegetius Renatus's work illustrates the same problems almost 2,000 years ago.

Five hundred years before Flavius Vegetius Renatus, General Sun Tzu Wu recorded what he had learned about warfare in the now famous booklet, *The Art of War*, where he also emphasized the importance of discipline. Historian Lionel Giles tells that Sun Tzu once won a battle with 30,000 soldiers against a force of 200,000 because the vanquished were undisciplined.[2] According to Sun Tzu, a general should know six situations that point to the defeat of an army:

- when soldiers take flight
- when they have lax discipline
- when the army is bogged down by weak soldiers
- when it collapses under insurgence
- when it is disorganized
- when it is routed

All of these situations are the result of poor discipline, and as Sun Tzu says, they "are the faults of the generals."[3]

Both of these historical examples teach the timeless lesson that the way to discipline soldiers is to train hard, develop physical and technical skills, communicate well, provide physical needs (e.g., food, clothing, rest), and instill pride through teamwork and respect for leaders. The wisdom continues in the modern U.S. Army, which places great importance on the tangible and intangible aspects of discipline. Every aspect of a soldier's life relates in some way to discipline in skills training, physical development, confidence building, teamwork, education, and self-control.

Discipline's Role in the Workplace

Good discipline can also make a difference in corporate success. The physically demanding training methods used by the Army to instill discipline may not be suitable for many businesses, but corporate leaders want the same kind of results as they prepare to meet the competition.

> "The discipline which makes the soldiers of a free country reliable in battle is not to be gained by harsh or tyrannical treatment. On the contrary, such treatment is far more likely to destroy than to make an army. . . . He who feels the respect which is due to others cannot fail to inspire in them regard for himself, while he who feels, and hence manifests, disrespect toward others, especially his inferiors, cannot fail to inspire hatred against himself."
>
> **—U.S. Army Major John Schofield in his 1879 address to cadets at the U.S. Military Academy, West Point, New York[4]**

Business leaders cannot operate in an environment where every individual must be told what to do and how to do it. Some jobs need this kind of supervision, but overall, businesses need people who can perform without detailed supervision of every move. And this is where discipline pays off.

Well-disciplined employees take it upon themselves to do a good job. When they understand what the company needs or what their supervisor would do, they take the initiative to do what is right for the company. Some of the characteristics you will observe among well-disciplined employees are as follows:

- They are on time for meetings and comply with standard work schedules.
- They stay until the job is finished.
- They use their initiative to get things done.
- They have a can-do attitude.
- They cooperate with team members and other departments.
- They pay attention to details so work is done properly.
- They remain enthusiastic during difficult times.
- They look for ways to improve performance.
- They suggest traditional and innovative ways to increase company profits.
- They avoid scheduling time off during peak business seasons.
- They persist even when they don't feel like being at work.
- They embrace change and undertake new training with enthusiasm.

Employees who exhibit these characteristics and others like them are truly disciplined and a great asset to the company. The positive attitude of well-disciplined employees makes it much easier to control stress in the workplace, while undisciplined employees create negative stress by failing in key areas such as those just listed.

Is Your Business Disciplined?

Army field manual FM 22-100, *Army Leadership*,[5] describes seven key leadership values that are always demonstrated by well-disciplined soldiers. The more disciplined soldiers are, the closer they align with these values. Naturally, this statement is true for employees and companies as well. The Army uses the acronym *LDRSHIP* to facilitate easy recall of the seven values:

1. Loyalty
2. Duty
3. Respect
4. Selfless service
5. Honor
6. Integrity
7. Personal courage

To determine the level of discipline in your company, consider how closely individuals line up with these leadership values, regardless of the person's rank.

Loyalty

By definition, loyalty means unswerving allegiance to a person, an institution, or a cause. You can count on loyal individuals when times are tough or when extra effort is required. You know that loyal people will support fellow team members. Even at their personal expense, loyal employees do what is right for their team, their organization, and their country.

> "Bear true faith and allegiance to the U.S. Constitution, the Army, and other soldiers."
>
> **—Army field manual FM 22-100, *Army Leadership***

Loyalty is a two-way affair, however. Leaders who are not loyal to their subordinates will find little loyalty in the ranks. *Army Leadership* explains, "The loyalty of your people is a gift they give you when, and only when, you deserve it—when you train them well, treat them fairly, and live by the concepts you talk about. Leaders who are loyal to their subordinates never let them be misused."

In *Army Leadership* General John Wickham, chief of staff of the U.S. Army in the 1980s, states that "Trust is the cornerstone of loyalty. If our subordinates, comrades, and superiors trust us, loyalty follows easily." You can show your own loyalty by doing things like giving credit to subordinates for the things they accomplish; taking responsibility for things that go wrong in your area, even when a subordinate makes the error; and rewarding your team well with annual pay raises, preferred time off, and a good share of your own time so they know you care about them.

Duty

This characteristic of self-discipline is revealed when one always does more than is expected with a sense of pride in a job well done, a joy that comes from helping others, and a humble understanding that the job is important, no matter how insignificant it might seem. They understand the intentions of their leaders and carry through even when unsupervised. They know right from wrong and do the right thing regardless of the personal cost.

> "Fulfill your obligations."
>
> **—Army field manual FM 22-100, *Army Leadership***

By their own performance, well-disciplined leaders inspire a sense of duty in people. For these leaders, responsibility and trust are a major part of the process, the decision making, and the organization. If the leader trusts his or her employees, they will exceed all of his or her expectations. If leaders try to control every decision and every movement, employees will allow them to do so. Excessive management erodes a sense of duty and creates unnecessary stress.

Respect

Combat soldiers often find themselves in danger because they willingly follow orders or place themselves at risk protecting fellow soldiers. This type of respect and discipline does not come overnight. It is earned as dedicated leaders consistently demonstrate their own respect for the soldiers, providing equal opportunities and fair treatment to all.

"Duty, Honor, Country"

"Those three hallowed words reverently dictate what you want to be, what you can be, what you will be. They are your rallying point to build courage when courage seems to fail, to regain faith when there seems to be little cause for faith, to create hope when hope becomes forlorn."

—General Douglas MacArthur's speech to the Corps of Cadets at the U.S. Military Academy at West Point, NY, May 12, 1962, in accepting the Thayer Award

Treating people with respect does not mean going easy on them. Instead, it means expecting the best of them while treating them with courtesy, honesty, and trust. Leaders need the respect of employees, especially in hard times, and employees perform at their best if they have the respect of the leaders. When employees respect their leaders, they are enthusiastic about work assignments and cooperate in every way possible to achieve corporate goals. As the workload and positive stress increase, their productivity goes right up. Disrespectful leaders, on the other hand, create a lot of negative stress and productivity goes down.

"Treat people as they should be treated."

—Army field manual FM 22-100, *Army Leadership*

Selfless Service

Selfless service means putting the interests of the nation and others ahead of one's own self-centered ambitions. Strong teams develop when leaders and soldiers put others' interests ahead of their own. Organizations are stronger when every member of the team strives to be of service to others.

Service becomes even more important the higher you climb on the ladder of success. The more rank you have, the more you must be of service to your subordinates. Surprise the people in your office today. Put your "urgent" projects aside, and ask team members what you can do to help them get their work done. Find out what is really happening in the ranks. Demonstrate your willingness to work alongside your team members. Visit the remote places where they do not expect you.

> "Put the welfare of the nation, the Army, and subordinates before your own."
>
> **—Army field manual FM 22-100, *Army Leadership***

Leaders who demonstrate their selfless service by visiting the front lines build the respect and loyalty of their troops. They get a firsthand understanding of the action. They enhance the discipline of the unit.

Like the other values, selfless service is something you must demonstrate daily. People believe their observations more than your words on this subject, and your selfless service will be influential in teaching others this trait while reducing stress in the workplace.

> "The nation today needs men who think in terms of service to their country and not in terms of their country's debt to them."
>
> **—General Omar Bradley**

Honor

As a key element of both leadership and discipline, dictionaries define honor as "a keen sense of ethical conduct"[6] and a "principled uprightness of character and personal integrity."[7] *Army Leadership* explains honor by incorporating all of the other Army values: loyalty, duty, respect, selfless service, integrity, and personal courage. Honor is a summation of these values, and it is manifested in action.

As an example of this value, the Army's leadership manual describes two sergeants who gave their lives trying to rescue a downed helicopter pilot in Mogadishu, Somalia, in 1993. Master Sergeant Gary Gordon and Sergeant First Class Randall Shugart requested permission three times before being allowed to drop from another helicopter to defend the injured pilot. After gaining permission, they fought their way to the helicopter and defended the pilot until his rescue. Both sergeants died of the wounds they received and posthumously received the Medal of Honor for their selfless service. They gave their all, remaining loyal to their fellow soldier, doing their duty, and demonstrating their personal courage in the face of great danger.

> "Live up to all the Army values."
>
> **—Army field manual FM 22-100, Army Leadership**

In civilian life, the community and their peers recognize honorable people. They are examples to others as they conduct their lives based upon these values. They are self-disciplined, and they motivate others to follow their lead. Leaders with honor can instill this spirit in their organization to enhance discipline and success.

> "What is life without honor? Degradation is worse than death."
>
> **—Lieutenant General Thomas J. "Stonewall" Jackson**

Undisciplined people lack this sense of honor. They hardly have a kind word for others, much less would they be willing to give their lives to help someone else. They can be recognized by the way they talk about others and cheat the company. When the going gets tough and they are needed most, these undisciplined, dishonorable people take flight.

However, people who have a high sense of honor are well disciplined and confident in themselves and their organization. During times of high stress, they help stabilize the situation and encourage others.

Integrity

Many successful people wish for integrity. Yet concession after concession has eroded their integrity until they can no longer make decisions based on right and wrong. Their entire organizations suffer the consequences of leadership without integrity.

> "Do what's right—legally and morally."
>
> **—Army field manual FM 22-100, *Army Leadership***

Great discipline is required for organizational leaders to avoid any hint of deviating from doing the right thing in their private and public lives. Others are watching, and the smallest deviation gives them permission to choose the wrong course themselves.

In the first three years of the new millennium, one major company after the other toppled because of wrongdoing at the top. Management lost its integrity. Shareholders lost their life savings. Employees lost jobs. The American public lost confidence in corporate leadership.

> "The American people rightly look to their military leaders to be skilled in the profession of arms and to be men of integrity."
>
> **—General J. Lawton Collins**

The press and the courts blamed these fallen leaders for greed, corruption, and theft. By most standards, the accused were titans of commerce, captains of industry, and leaders of American business empires. Cracks in their integrity caused their wrongdoing or exposed them to these accusations.

Army Leadership would tell these leaders that people of integrity do the right thing not because it's convenient or because they have no choice. They choose the right thing because their character permits no less. Conducting yourself with integrity has three parts:

1. Separating what's right from what's wrong
2. Always acting according to what you know to be right, even at personal cost

3. Saying openly that you're acting on your understanding of
   right versus wrong (to make sure others understand and learn
   from your position of integrity)[8]

My own military training taught me early on that I must always
choose the harder right instead of the easier wrong. It became a part
of my character, and when I found myself confronted by hard decisions in my military and corporate careers, the decision was already
in place. I had made the decision years before to choose right, regardless of the personal circumstances. By making the decision ahead of
time, I removed the emotional element in making decisions. No matter how tempting it was to choose the easier wrong, I could confidently move forward with my integrity intact.

When I speak on this subject, I remind audiences that the consequences of doing right are only temporary. The consequences of doing
wrong will last a lifetime and beyond. Even if the consequences seem
overwhelming, you have the satisfaction of knowing that you did the
right thing. Your stress will be positive. Otherwise, knowing that you
did the wrong thing might be overwhelming, and there is no way to
reverse the decision. The negative stress accompanying a decidedly
wrong action is persistent and debilitating.

So how do you build integrity into your ranks? How does it
become a part of a disciplined organization? The answer lies in making the decision ahead of time and in demonstrating utmost integrity
at every turn.

Personal Courage

Combat presents opportunities to display physical courage, but
opportunities exist every day for leaders, soldiers, and employees to
display moral courage. Courage is required for people to stand firm
on their principles and convictions and do the right thing. Courage
is necessary for people to admit they are wrong or to change course
after they have announced a position. Discipline is an essential part
of this courage.

It will surprise some to discover that *Army Leadership* also teaches soldiers about the moral courage required to express their thoughts when it might seem easier to remain silent. Subordinates learn objectivity in disagreeing with policies and actions, and leaders learn objectivity in correcting subordinates' errors. The training literature explains that this candor is essential for trust between leaders and subordinates.

"Face fear, danger, or adversity— physical or moral."

—Army field manual FM 22-100, *Army Leadership*

Soldiers learn about moral courage in both the classroom and by example, but they learn physical courage through realistic training and confidence building. The early morning runs, obstacle courses, and physical training are much more than harassment or making soldiers physically fit. These events are the first steps in strengthening discipline and building physical courage. Both individual events and team events encourage self-discipline by subjecting one's own interests to those of the team. If soldiers display courage, their confidence increases and that causes their stress levels to decrease.

Training in the arena of moral courage is just as important for businesses. Young leaders need to understand the morals and ethics of senior management so they can reinforce these important characteristics with all employees. You can coach leaders in their decision making so they will understand the importance of doing the right thing despite the personal and corporate cost. You can also demonstrate your own moral courage by encouraging and accepting feedback when they think you are wrong in your actions.

Every company has leaders and employees who are courageous, and they can be examples for everyone. Leaders can teach moral courage in both informal conversation and in formal training as companies try to deal with situational ethics, *multiple truths*, and opportunities to make wrong decisions. In addition to reading assignments and classes, you can engage leaders in conversation about their responses to various ethical dilemmas. Draw on your own experiences for these conversations so the subject will be relevant and revealing. Tell them how you have handled situations and ask how they would react. People who lack discipline in this area are vulnerable to the effects of negative stress that accompany every challenge to their moral courage. Those with weak moral courage find themselves stressed in having to make decisions between doing what is right and what will advance them personally, and a string of greedy decisions erodes confidence, causing even further stress.

Personal courage might receive high priority in your company if you know it is required to develop the other values needed for strong discipline. British political leader Sir Winston Churchill concluded that "Courage is the first of human qualities because it is the quality which guarantees all others."

Discipline and Leadership

Self-discipline and team discipline are both required for success on the battlefield and in the marketplace. Since ancient times, people have known that disciplined teams are much more likely to succeed than are teams lacking the values described in this chapter.

The marketplace is not the same as a military battlefield, but employees do feel the pinch of defeat with corporate downsizing, cutbacks, and closings. Now is a good time to take a hard look at your company and determine whether you have the leadership and discipline to survive into the future. The next chapter looks at how the Army executes plans, as you consider what you need to do with your team.

Notes

1. Flavius Vegetius Renatus, *The Military Institutions of the Romans (De re militari)*, translated from the Latin by Lieutenant John Clarke. Text written in A.D. 390, British translation in 1767.
2. Lionel Giles, *Sun Tzu on* The Art of War, Luzac and Co. in London and Shanghai, 1910.
3. Ibid.

4. Army field manual FM 22-100, *Army Leadership*, Headquarters, Department of the Army, Washington, D.C., August 31, 1999.

5. Army field manual FM 22-100, *Army Leadership*, is the source of the leadership values, quotations, examples, and points of discussion in this chapter.

6. The American Heritage Dictionary of the English Language, Fourth Edition, 2000.

7. Dictionary.com.

8. FM 22-100, *Army Leadership*.

13

THE ELEMENT OF SURPRISE

★

Even if the enemy knows of your plans, the element of surprise can lead to victory as it did for the United States in World War I. The United States first declared war on Germany in April 1917, and within a month General John J. (Black Jack) Pershing was in France with more than half a million soldiers. Initially, a few elements of the American Expeditionary Force (AEF) fought under the command of the French and British armies, but by early autumn, General Pershing convinced them to allow an American-led task force against St. Mihiel, a city in northeastern France and a critical point in the four-year-old German line of defense.

News of the attack was leaked to the press, and a Swiss paper actually announced the planned time and location of the opening barrage. German commanders thought they understood the plans, but they didn't anticipate the additional, simultaneous flanking attacks planned by Black Jack Pershing. Before mid-afternoon of D-day,[1] the AEF broke through the first defensive positions. By the end of the second day, the AEF was deep into the *impregnable* line of defense. A French force of more than a hundred thousand soldiers attacked through the breach at St. Mihiel, and the Allied armies continued eastward into Verdun and the Argonne Forest, signaling the beginning of Allied victories that led to Germany's defeat fourteen months later.[2]

Even though Germany had known of the impending attack, they were surprised by General Pershing's combat tactics and the size of the American force concentrated on a relatively small front.[3] A good solid plan and the element of surprise took the Allies from stress to success when they broke the line of defense that others had found impenetrable for years.

Plan for Action

Extensive plans do not guarantee success, but the absence of plans for action almost guarantees failure. General Pershing's operations plan at St. Mihiel was only seven pages long, but its clarity ensured that all subordinate commanders understood what must be done. The French plan, on the other hand, was more than a hundred fifty pages,[4] and they had spent four years across the trenches from the German occupation force. American commanders understood their objectives, knew the cities and villages along key routes, and recognized how momentum was essential once the battle began.

Unlike the AEF strategy, however, the German plan included instructions to retreat if the Americans threatened to envelop the frontline units. Both forces achieved their plans. Actually, the Germans did not have a plan of *action* at St. Mihiel; instead, they only had a plan to react to AEF maneuvers.

Companies that plan for success stand a much better chance of getting there than those who have no plan at all or, worse yet, those who plan for failure as the Germans did. There are exceptions, of course, but businesses where sales and profits remain stagnant year after year might be suffering from the German "no action" plan syndrome where everyone works hard but nothing gets done. The entire staff of no-action companies focus on reacting to competitors who would like to put them out of business. Everyone is frustrated and stress is overwhelming because they lack control of the situation, and they are tired of working with no end in sight and no plan to succeed.

Good solid plans help alleviate stress, clear minds, and set directions. Good plans call for action—the action required to achieve the goals.

The Importance of Surprise

Pershing's plan included the nine principles of war discussed in Chapter 10, and it also included surprise as its key element in shifting the balance of power. If your company wants to use the element of surprise to knock competitors off balance and gain market share, you will want to consider each of the following six factors that the Army finds important.

Six Factors of Surprise

1. Speed
2. Intelligence
3. Deception
4. Combat Power
5. Security
6. Variations

Speed

Speed is essential to companies in responding to customer needs, corporate decision-making, manufacturing, quality corrections, product introductions, modifications, news releases, public relations, crisis control, communications, special training, price adjustments, technological change, adding personnel, financial investments, loan acquisition, alliances, distribution, and any other action that gives you an advantage over competitors. You can increase your company's speed in each of these areas by planning and practicing. It will do you no good to be the first on the scene, however, if you have all the wrong information and ill-conceived proposals.

Intelligence

Sophisticated companies know the importance of analyzing information about competitors, suppliers, and markets, while other companies just collect whatever information they stumble upon and hope to make something of it. Without analysis, the information they gather is useless in competitive efforts. Unfortunately, some corporate leaders don't even gather the data needed for participating in the marketplace.

A conscientious effort is required to collect, systematize, analyze, and distribute intelligence to those who can make use of it. The victor knows more than the competition does. They know what the information means, and they have plans for using the intelligence gained in the analysis. Whoever accomplishes this process first gains the surprise and beats the competition.

My first encounter with corporate intelligence gathering was at the Pittsburgh, Pennsylvania, headquarters of Alcoa. As our company's sales team prepared for the visit to Alcoa to announce a price increase, we researched our sales information for Alcoa: current price, price history, and order history for the past five years. We talked about our own cost of manufacturing and the need for additional revenue. We were ready to announce the price increase.

Within minutes of being seated at their conference table, however, we discovered we actually were very unprepared for the visit. Alcoa knew more than we did about our company's position, and they refused to accept a price increase. After we explained the reasons for the price adjustment, Alcoa purchasing agents politely gave us a lesson in corporate intelligence. Their impromptu use of notebooks, charts, graphs, reference materials, and media information was extensive. Not only did they know about our company, they knew about every influence on the raw materials and manufacturing processes several layers up the supply chain.

To make matters even more embarrassing, the purchasing team had a junior member explain the specifics of their decision to decline the price increase. Here is what they had:

Information About Our Company
- Transportation costs for our raw materials, and packing and shipping expenses
- Our total annual production volume for the product they purchased—rather accurate

- Electric power costs, a key ingredient of our reason for the price increase, including historical media information on our earlier negotiations with the electric providers
- Labor costs, average for our area plus the costs of fringe benefits
- The number of employees working in our plants that produced their products
- The average cost per square foot of leased corporate headquarters office space
- Our major customers and estimates of their annual usage and price of similar products
- Corporate net profits from previous years and the last quarter
- The amount of bad debt written off in the previous year
- Insurance costs and retirement plan investments
- Our cost of sales calls and other overhead included in the price
- Our company president's publicly announced goals for the year and his near-term personal plans

Information About Our Suppliers
- Our sources of raw materials used in making the product Alcoa purchased
- Major customers of each of those sources
- Average cost of these raw materials in our market—and in others!
- Specifics that drive the production costs among our suppliers—labor, equipment, transportation
- Plans for expansion and contraction in those industries
- Impact of union negotiations and strikes
- Key management personnel—background, strengths, and weaknesses
- Vendors who provided the raw materials and supplies to our sources
- Key factors that influenced the costs of our sources' raw materials

Information About the Marketplace
- Industry trends
- Shortages and overages in manufacturing capacity
- Total industry-wide inventory
- New uses for our products and similar products
- State and federal congressional actions that would influence manufacturing and supply
- Impact of Environmental Protection Agency activities on products and their use
- Impact of the monetary exchange rate on imports and exports
- Annual production volume of offshore suppliers

Their surprise was very effective. Alcoa refused the price increase even though other customers accepted our explanation without a challenge. Alcoa purchasing managers collected all of this information from public sources, and they had analyzed it to determine how each item affected their costs in that budget year. They had also distributed the analysis to key purchasing and production managers. When they finished the lesson that afternoon, we not only agreed with them but left quickly to avoid talking about a price reduction rather than an increase.

You can gather this type of information yourself, or you can hire consultants and firms to do the footwork for you. Everything in Alcoa's list is public information. It is in the media, annual reports, brochures, quarterly federal reports, conversations with sales reps and suppliers, fellow purchasing agents, trade show information, trade journals, government reports, and customers. Customers, suppliers, salespeople, and trade associations all have valuable information to help identify trends. Intelligence of this depth will help you understand your own suppliers and marketplace, and it can help you justify your price increases to your major customers. This kind of knowledge might help you surprise your competitors as well.

Remember, you do not have to be unethical or illegal to gather any of the important information about your competition, suppliers, or customers. Just pay attention, assemble the information, and analyze it. Properly used, this kind of intelligence can also be of use internally as you prepare budgets, hiring plans, sales strategies, financing proposals, equipment purchases, and construction projects.

You will make a big hit with your supervisors and have a major impact on productivity if you collect and analyze this type of information. Intelligence alone can help you turn your plans into action. Managers and employees take great comfort in knowing their leadership is well informed and prepared to maximize their company's position.

Deception

Just as the military uses deception to trick its enemies, deception works in the corporate marketplace. For example, competitors who misunderstand your true intentions are surprised when they expect a product to come to market and you suddenly or secretly withdraw it.

At one time, our sales team gained significant advantage over a competitor who was deceived by our cross-country truck shipments to his West Coast customers. He had maintained a monopoly for years, and he knew that we were unable to compete because of distance and exorbitant freight costs. When he learned of our trial shipments, he accurately concluded that we could not serve these accounts by truck, and he made belligerent remarks about his monopoly.

The surprise came when he discovered that the trucks were deceptively concealing our real effort, which included rail shipments and West Coast distribution points. Before he could react, we were established. Within a year we had 40 percent of his market share, and within two years he was out of business. He took the fortune he had made on the monopoly and retired to the tropics. The void was filled with other competitors who followed our lead.

The nature of deception requires the confidence of key people, and leaders need to make sure everyone differentiates between permissible deception and deception that will land them in jail. Understated expenses, overstated asset values, misleading new product information, and other such deceptive practices are all illegal. Deception of shareholders can be fatal to the company and those managers involved. Neither leaders nor employees admire illegal deception, but all of them appreciate the additional business that comes when competitors misunderstand what is going on in the marketplace.

Combat Power

Once you understand your objectives, use all of your resources to overwhelm the competition. Every part of your company should be involved in helping you reach those objectives. Companies with divisiveness among its divisions experience a loss of net profits, but those with joint efforts and the combined horsepower of cooperating divisions can overwhelm the competition. Separate divisions can often lower costs by cooperating to bring a product to market. The sharing of transportation, warehousing, administrative, and accounting resources can significantly strengthen a sales effort. Corporations who understand this principle certainly surprise competitors and firm up their market share. This is combat power in action.

Alliances between individual companies can also enhance combat power and increase sales for everyone involved, sometimes saving money for the customers as well. Teaming up with vendors and sources surprises competitors and puts them in an uncompetitive position. For example, at one point I established a favorable alliance with another company and the railroad to reduce freight costs to many customers who bought from both companies. The two of us agreed to inventory each other's products, and the railroad gave a price concession because of the additional business. Competitors for both companies were surprised when we took some of their major accounts.

The combat power of cooperative sales teams can also add the element of surprise needed to throw the competition off balance. Corporations with multiple divisions do not always direct a cooperative effort among the separate sales teams. But those teams who have good relationships with buyers can maximize their corporate combat power by sharing the relationships with other sales teams. The sharing of relationships might be so valuable that you would want to share commissions with those who help you open the door with a client.

Focusing combat power surprises competitors and can be a great advantage for those who understand it. Also, by reducing uncertainty, success after success lowers stress levels everywhere—except with the competition.

Security

Traditional security measures probably come as no surprise to competitors. They are more likely to be surprised, however, when other companies do not guard their own operations.

I was sure surprised when our sales representative submitted a handwritten list of current competitive prices offered to our largest customer. The purchasing agent had been especially careful to avoid telling us the prices, but the competing sales representative helped greatly when he left the proposal lying on the dash of his car. Our sales rep read the key information right through the windshield. Don't surprise the competition by giving them the information they need. Furthermore, don't be surprised if competitors give you misinformation. The information must be analyzed before it becomes intelligence.

Instead of giving competitors the information they want, surprise them by withholding information from the marketplace. If they are accustomed to picking up your prices from customers, surprise them by developing customer-supplier nondisclosure agreements in exchange for lower prices or some other advantage to the customers. My customers appreciated the nondisclosure agreements so much they negotiated even more business, with our offer of an end-of-year bonus if they succeeded in withholding information from the competition. The competition was very surprised when their good friends refused to give them a hint of the deal we made. The competition's price cuts and sales maneuvers never became quite good enough to make up for the package proposal we tendered.

You can also surprise the competition by guarding media information. If the competition is accustomed to following your every move in the local newspaper, change the timing on news releases. To make this principle most effective, you have to understand how competitors get information about your company. Their methods are probably not very sophisticated, but the better you understand them, the better you can surprise competitors. Make it part of your intelligence-gathering effort. You should also do a better job than my company did with Alcoa.

Variations

One of the best ways to surprise competitors is simply to vary the way you do business. They know your preferred method of negotiating new business. They know how and when you raise prices, and how much you are usually willing to retract. But varying your shipping schedules, billing discounts, sales call pattern, customer service techniques, purchasing, and inventory can all throw the competition off schedule. If your salespeople have routine team meetings on a certain schedule, change it. Call on their customers when you usually would be in a meeting. Instead of using Friday afternoons for administrative catch-up work, take customers on special relationship-building outings. Let competitors stay in the office thinking that customers don't want to see anyone on Friday afternoons.

If others know your purchasing pattern, do something different. By using my competitor's own news release to disrupt his importing business, I once prevented him from taking 25 percent of my market share. When he announced his import schedule to gain customer interest, we simply adjusted prices to make his "special" offer much less attractive. Our lower special prices kept customers long enough to cause the importer big financing problems. In the end, he dumped the goods at a loss and stayed away from our customers.

If you decide to use variations to surprise competitors, be sure to coordinate the effort within your own company. The other managers and employees don't like surprises any more than you do. Include plenty of time in your planning to educate employees and to test the strategy. Otherwise, you will create additional stress for yourself and everyone involved.

Leadership in Action

Companies can get bogged down in reacting to competitive threats. Just like the Allied forces in France, you can spend years responding to the competition while your market share stagnates or spirals downward. The stress created by this stagnation can be seen in arguments between sales and support people about quality, production schedules, distribution, accounting, and customer service. The stress causes a general lack of cooperation among all of these departments. Even your customers feel the stress in their relationships with your people.

You can tackle all of these problems at one time by breaking out of the status quo and going on the attack. Just like the Allied forces at St. Mihiel, you can use the element of surprise to shift the balance of power and gain market share. Consider each principle of war as you get your entire company involved in the effort, and let them share your renewed confidence as you prepare to break through competitive defenses. The competition will probably be surprised by the mere fact that you are breaking away from the routine they've come to expect, and your calculated attack can revive the enthusiasm of everyone involved.

Just as with any other effort to reduce stress, leadership is a key factor in putting plans into action as well as gaining the victory itself. Chapter 14 takes a closer look at leadership in the Army and offers comparisons with corporate leadership challenges.

Notes

1. *D-day* is Army shorthand for the start date of a designated operation. *Combat Orders*, Fort Leavenworth, Kansas: The General Service Schools Press, 1922.
2. John J. Pershing, "Description of the Battle of St. Mihiel," *Final Report of General John J. Pershing*, Washington, D.C.: Government Printing Office, 1919.
3. Douglas MacArthur, George S. Patton, Billy Mitchell, and Eddie Rickenbacker all played key roles in the battle at St. Mihiel.
4. Pershing, "Description of the Battle of St. Mihiel."

14

LEADERSHIP

★

───────────────────────────────────────

Throughout *Winning Under Fire* you have seen that skilled leaders are good at controlling stress in their organizations. Corporate leaders channel positive stress into improved performance and higher profits, and military leaders do the same to guarantee victory on the battlefield. Many of the characteristics that ensure success also help leaders control stress and get the best from their people.

Previous chapters have already discussed the principles of war and other important tools that great leaders use, but the question remains as to just what it takes to be a successful combat leader. To answer this question, some dedicated Army officers analyzed various battles and recorded the essential elements for success in Army field manual FM 3-0, *Fundamentals of Full Spectrum Operations*:

- Initiative
- Agility
- Depth
- Synchronization
- Versatility

This chapter shows how great leaders use these elements to guide their people to victory.

Initiative

Army commanders make every effort to remain on the offensive because experience has shown that this is the way to win wars. Even when defensive tactics are necessary, commanders and soldiers try to use the offensive to control the battle space. Strong commanders know that controlling the battlefield and the surrounding areas of influence (air, communications, technology, logistics, etc.) can give them freedom of action while limiting the enemy's ability to maneuver.

Definition: setting or dictating the terms of action throughout the battle or operation

—**Army field manual**
FM 3-0, *Fundamentals of Full Spectrum Operations*

Good corporate leaders enjoy this same kind of freedom by applying their own *initiative*. They can do this by structuring their organization to outpace competitors in introducing products, assisting customers, and influencing the marketplace. They shorten the decision-making process and delegate responsibilities so they can react to competitive situations faster than competitors.

General Dwight D. Eisenhower and the World War II Allied Assault at Normandy

When Germany launched their 1939 offensive against Western Europe, the British were defeated badly at Dunkirk and driven back to England. Other countries such as Denmark, Holland, Belgium, Luxembourg, and France fell quickly, and Germany soon occupied the continent. It took two and a half years for the Allies to launch an offensive across the beaches of Normandy to regain the initiative lost in the early days of World War II.

With agreement from all the Allies, President Roosevelt named General Dwight D. Eisenhower as Supreme Commander in this bold assault against the well-established German army. Allied leaders chose England as the staging ground, and more than a million and a half American troops were gathered there.

To prevent German air reconnaissance from discovering their real plans, Allied leaders constructed an elaborate deception that included a phantom navy made of rubber boats and facades made to look like barracks. A communications network was established to fill the air with phony messages, and an air assault was directed against an alternative landing site at Pas de Calais, France, instead of the true destination on the beaches of Normandy. When airborne troops parachuted behind enemy lines to disrupt reinforcements that Germany might send to Normandy, Hitler was firmly convinced that the main attack would come at Pas de Calais. Just as planned, this massive deception was a key factor in disrupting the balance of power and gaining the initiative on the entire western front.

Individual initiative proved to be just as important as soldiers fought their way across the beaches, up the cliffs, and through the hedgerows where the Germans resisted their every step forward. Situations changed rapidly, and individuals acted independently as they fought toward their objectives. They could not wait for instructions from headquarters before responding to German gunfire and shifting positions. They had to take the initiative at every turn.

The Importance of Corporate Initiative

Gaining the initiative might seem impossible to corporate leaders who have long been on the defensive. Their lack of initiative keeps them from envisioning the overthrow of well-established competitors. There seems to be some safety in defending the small market share they have and a great deal of risk in going after competitors' business.

In truth, however, the defensive positions they occupy are far more dangerous than being on the offensive. Those who wish to maintain the status quo are in danger of defeat. Competitors try to take business away from those companies that simply defend their market share. Elaborate defenses without some offensive initiative will cause these companies on the defense to collapse just as the Germans lost their hold on the western front.

Corporate leaders must continue the assault whenever they deliver a blow to a competitor. Competitors need to be kept off balance, because they do not like losing market share and they will counter-attack as quickly as they can consolidate their forces and plan their move. Keep the pressure on competitors with surprise after surprise and give them no chance to restabilize their forces.

When a company is on the defensive and only responding to competitive attacks, stress reactions tend to be negative. In addition to complaining about the competitor, employees start to complain about their own company's managers, people, and products. Tensions rise as the defensive company feels they have no control over the situation. If your people demonstrate these and other symptoms of stress, you can turn it all around by going on the attack. Maintaining the initiative and attacking competitors can help you control stress and encourage positive reactions throughout your company.

Agility

Agile leaders react faster than their opponents. They quickly grasp the essence of unfamiliar situations and understand the action required. They seize the initiative and exploit any advantage gained in the attack. Military and corporate leaders demonstrate their agility by shifting tactics and resources to meet unexpected situations, changing from the offense to the defense quickly and using available resources.

> Definition: the ability to move and adjust quickly and easily
>
> —**Army field manual**
> **FM 3-0**, *Fundamentals of Full Spectrum Operations*

President Roosevelt and General MacArthur

In late December 1941, just weeks after Pearl Harbor and the simultaneous destruction of the U.S. airpower at Clark Field in the Philippines, Japanese forces surrounded Corregidor Island and seemed ready to overrun both the Filipinos and General MacArthur's headquarters. President Roosevelt understood the dangers involved and ordered MacArthur to break through the Japanese lines and escape to Australia. MacArthur and his family made the 2,400-mile journey aboard aging PT boats, Army aircraft, and the Australian railroad. En route MacArthur explained to reporters that the president ordered him out of the Philippines to organize the American offensive against Japan, and Filipinos took hope from his famous last words in that speech when MacArthur said, "I will return."[1]

> Operational agility "is not merely physical; it requires conceptual sophistication and intellectual flexibility."
>
> **—Army field manual FM 3-0, *Fundamentals of Full Spectrum Operations***

President Roosevelt's actions illustrate the principle of operational agility at the highest level. He knew the capture of MacArthur would be a significant loss to America and the war effort as well as a huge propaganda victory for the Japanese. While the decision was unpopular with some in the press and the 15,000 Americans left behind in the Philippines, Roosevelt's orders saved the leader who could bring together American forces to attack the Japanese a year and a half later and win back the territory for the Filipino people.

During MacArthur's subsequent troop buildup, when Japan controlled nearly 15 percent of the globe and military strategists predicted a ten-year war to recapture territory in the Pacific, General MacArthur undertook a campaign to "hit 'em where they ain't."[2] Choosing less-defended islands, the Americans conducted sixteen amphibious landings with speed and surprise to establish beachheads closer and closer to the Philippines. America's 1944 assault against the Japanese in the Philippines was another demonstration of tactical agility, as soldiers fought through machine-gun-infested swamps and over highly defended mountains, attacking and withdrawing to maneuver and gain ground. Stories of heroism abound as tenacious American soldiers refused to give up this hard-won territory.

At times, agile commanders and frontline soldiers withdraw to avoid unnecessary losses and then attack again to exploit enemy weaknesses. Ultimately, the agility of these commanders and their troops contributed to the defeat of the well-disciplined and highly trained Japanese soldiers.

Corporate leaders can be as agile as Army commanders if they are willing to apply the principles of war and the elements of successful operations. In unfamiliar circumstances, business leaders must understand how to gain advantage of competitors by acting and reacting before they lose market share. More-complacent business leaders take the easy path to defend what they have or they accept only modest gains. But agile leaders attack when there is a weakness and withdraw when competitor strength is overwhelming. If one way is blocked, they try another. They gain territory and exploit every small victory. Agile and determined leaders aggressively pursue every avenue for success regardless of the personal sacrifice, the work required, or the length of time involved. They do not accept defeat as final. They envision success and employ all resources to achieve their goals.

Those leaders who worry that their employees are too resistant toward frequent change need to introduce the concept of agility and explain how it can be used to their advantage. The reverses and corrections will be much less stressful if the employees understand how these frequent changes are actually well-thought-out tactical moves.

Depth

A study of great victories shows that the victors used all of the time, space, and resources available to them. They didn't limit themselves to engaging the enemy on the front line or at a set time of battle. They started the fight long before they engaged the enemy, and they attacked deep into enemy territory instead of just shooting at the soldiers in the foxholes. As *Fundamentals of Full Spectrum Operations* explains it, employment of depth

> Definition: the extension of operations in time, space, and resources
>
> **—Army field manual FM 3-0, *Fundamentals of Full Spectrum Operations***

gives commanders room for "effective maneuverability, time to conduct operations, and resources to achieve and exploit success."[3]

The depth of the battle begins long before D-day with efforts to gather intelligence about the enemy, interrupt logistical preparations, disrupt communications, and soften the psychological will to do battle. As the assault begins, joint operations include long-range and close air support, navy resources, and civilian assets to make an impact throughout the enemy's territory. The following example of General Norman Schwartzkopf excellently shows the leadership quality of depth.

General Norman Schwartzkopf and Desert Storm

For several weeks prior to the initial assault to drive Iraq out of Kuwait in January 1991, General Schwartzkopf used missiles and aircraft to soften Iraq's antiair weapons and missile capability. Then as the battle began, the U.S. Navy launched 388 Tomahawk Land Attack Missiles from cruisers, carriers, battleships, and submarines in the Red Sea and the Persian Gulf.[4] Coalition forces attacked targets throughout the country in addition to Iraqis on the front line. The joint air campaign involved aircraft from carriers in both the Red Sea and Persian Gulf as well as land-based aircraft from the region. U.S. Air Force sorties flew in from Western Europe and all the way from the United States to attack essential targets confronting coalition land forces.

According to Army historian, Brigadier General John Sloan Brown, the American logistics for Desert Storm were "striking." Logistical innovations included "state-of-the-art roll-on–roll-off shipping, modern containerization, an efficient single-fuel system, and automated information management."[5] The depth of the attack, the rapid destruction of everything needed for Iraq to sustain itself, and the overwhelming combat power brought victory in just 100 hours. The coalition forces pushed Iraq out of Kuwait and destroyed a significant amount of Iraq's military infrastructure.

Some corporate successes are limited because companies fail to use their resources in depth. If they only reduce prices, they will not likely gain market share for the long term. If they attack the competition with only a quick-ship program, they will not likely gain customers permanently. Companies can gain only a marginal level of success—unless they apply *depth* to their attack by using all possible resources: introducing alternative products, lowering prices, importing lower-cost supplies, acquiring automated equipment, reducing personnel, implementing quality management systems, improving marketing and advertising, doubling up on sales efforts, and so on.

In today's sophisticated market, winning companies coordinate their plan of attack to include all of these strategies and more. They use technology to gather competitive intelligence, develop sales, and deliver products. Expert project managers use their skills to help coordinate all a company's resources to attack in depth. The key to in-depth competition lies in planning for the use of every conceivable tool against every possible competitive target.

The victors of corporate battles are the companies that attack across a wide front and into the heart of competitors' operations. Instead of attacking a single product, leaders coordinate attacks against all of the competitor's products. Alliances are developed with other manufacturers and sales teams to disrupt every item in the competitor's product line. Prices are adjusted, costs reduced, quality improved, and relationships built. Vendor and supplier relationships are enhanced so competitors just can't get the same deals as those involved in the alliance. As I've cautioned elsewhere, you must coach all managers on the legality of their efforts. It makes no sense to break the law and risk losing the hard-won gains.

Synchronization

While depth indicates what the Army will do, synchronization indicates when and where things will happen. Synchronization involves prioritizing and sequencing events to maximize the effects of an attack plan. For synchronization to happen, each element of combat power must be applied at a precise place and precise time to maintain the initiative and overwhelm the enemy.

As seen in the examples from the Normandy landing and Desert Storm, some of the combat actions must take place before the main attack begins. In World War II, air attacks neutralized German rail, fuel, and air support before the Normandy landing began. In Desert Storm, electronic warfare was used to intercept Iraq's important radio communications, locate specific targets, identify the location of mobile weapons, and eliminate antiaircraft weapons systems. Some of these activities took place on the same ground that the coalition forces would later fight across, and other activities took place miles away. Synchronizing the priority and timing of the attacks was crucial in order to get the battlefield ready for ground troops and to demoralize the enemy command.

> Definition: arranging activities in time, space, and purpose to mass maximum relative combat power at a decisive place and time
>
> **—Army field manual FM 3-0, *Fundamentals of Full Spectrum Operations***

In the same way, corporate synchronization enhances business operations against competitors. Leaders can make sure to synchronize marketing and advertising with the release of new products and to keep close track of inventory levels and necessary manufacturing supplies. Leaders must also time the efforts of the sales team, attacking the competitors' products in the right order at the right accounts in the right markets. If the competitor's sales managers are occupied in defending certain offers, they will be less effective when their second and third products are attacked. Some customers are greater alarmists than others, so the timing of your offers to these companies needs to coincide with the competition's most stressful times.

A sound plan for synchronizing attacks against competitors improves chances for success. Informing employees of the plan decreases stress and increases confidence in their own well-being. Most employees feel a lot more comfortable when their company is growing than they do when it is on the defensive.

Don't forget to plan for competitive counterattacks. As you determine how the competition will respond to your synchronized, in-depth attack, make plans for what you will do about their reaction.

Versatility

The final element of success discovered to be present in battlefield victory is versatility in being able to meet the demands of worldwide threats of various kinds. The Army must be prepared to conduct various types of missions (combat and noncombat) in different climates. Just as units are qualified in more than one capability, individuals also must be cross-trained to maximize the chances of success. According to Army field manual FM 71-100, *Division Operations,* "Versatility is the ability to shift focus, to tailor forces, and to move from one mission to another rapidly and efficiently. It implies a capacity to be multifunctional, to operate across regions throughout the full range of military operations."

> Definition: the ability of Army forces to meet the global, diverse mission requirements of full spectrum operations
>
> **—Army field manual**
> **FM 3-0, *Fundamentals of Full Spectrum Operations***

General Tommy Franks and Iraqi Freedom

Iraqi Freedom transplanted thousands of U.S. military reservists and National Guard soldiers from their civilian jobs into the midst of combat. They were trained during peacetime and ready to fight. Citizen soldiers from all corporate ranks put on their uniforms and answered the call to defend freedom.

When Operation Iraqi Freedom began, these former CEOs, middle managers, and frontline corporate employees applied their military skills and fought their way north to Baghdad and beyond, where they found their versatility again challenged by the peacekeeping requirements that came in the wake of their sudden victory. A few days after defeating the enemy in full combat operations, these infantrymen, tankers, and combat support soldiers found themselves acting as policemen, guards, and crowd control troops.

Passing These Tenets to Your Team Members

If you can adapt as these Army leaders do, you will be much more successful in facing the competition and much less stressed in competitive encounters. Your ability to adapt will meet the ultimate challenge if you meet a competitor who uses these five elements of success against you. You need to prepare far in advance if you hope to survive these concerted attacks. If your team leaders are unaccustomed to taking the initiative, you need to begin training for use of this Army tenet. Explain what you expect and give them opportunities to use their initiative. Instead of asking you for permission to attack the competition, let your team leaders know that you expect them to act first and advise you later.

You can improve the agility of your team leaders by confronting them with changes in plans and priorities. Teach people and give them opportunities to practice their agility. Unless you explain what is going on and prepare people for this type of change, the negative stress reactions will outweigh the benefits. The stress of facing the enemy in battle or in a competitive corporate situation can have serious consequences if leaders are unprepared. Stress-induced errors in planning and execution can easily affect the outcome of operations. However, you can reduce the amount of stress and provide confident leadership by training team leaders to use the same tenets the Army uses based upon their study of major victories in combat.

Formal training, personal coaching, and practice can develop your team leaders' skills in these elements that the Army has found present in many of its major victories: initiative, agility, depth, synchronization, and versatility. Implementation of skills such as these will reverse the effects of negative stress in your company and lead to positive behaviors instead. Chapter 15 presents some of the specific positive behaviors that leaders can attain by using good stress-control techniques.

Notes

1. Kenneth Friedman, *Afternoon of the Rising Sun: The Battle of Lyete Gulf.* Novato, California: Presidio Press, 2001.

2. Heike Hasenauer, "Back to the Philippines," author and photojournalist for *Soldier* magazine. Vol. 49, No. 10, October 1994.

3. Army field manual FM 3-0, *Fundamentals of Full Spectrum Operations*, Headquarters, Department of the Army, Washington, D.C. June 14, 2001.

4. Edward C. Mann III, *Thunder and Lightning: Desert Storm and the Airpower Debates*. Maxwell AFB: Air University Press, 1995, 1-Q.

5. Brigadier General John Sloan Brown, "Desert Storm as History—and Prologue," *Army Magazine*, February 2001.

15

STRIVE FOR EXCELLENCE

★

As leaders strive for excellence, they can benefit from many positive stress reactions, but they must also protect themselves from the effects of negative stress. Leaders who strive for perfection are more likely to suffer the ill effects of stress than are those who simply strive to be better than the competition. Those who try to outplay the competition are very much like athletic team captains who want their team to win more than they want perfection in every aspect of the game. Perfection in certain areas might contribute to success, but perfection in every action is not required for the team to win. Leaders who await the perfect plan, the perfect set of circumstances, or the perfect employees, however, might watch business go to competitors who simply strive for excellence and move forward with partially completed plans or imperfect circumstances.

As leaders strive for victory, they can count on a number of positive stress reactions similar to those found in the heat of battle. In this chapter, you first look at positive stress reactions identified in the Army field manual FM 22-51, *Leaders' Manual for Combat Stress Control*,[1] and then you explore some of the ways that leaders themselves can avoid becoming victims of the same stress they are trying to control in everyone else.

Excellence and Positive Stress Reactions

United States involvement in Iraqi Freedom reminds us that combat is dangerous regardless of how well soldiers are trained and motivated. High-tech weapons and massive combat power overwhelmed well-prepared Iraqi defenses and drove the Iraqi army from the field. Nevertheless, plenty of stressors created negative responses—sandstorms, lack of hygiene, combat rations. But plenty of positive behaviors also resulted from positive stress:

- Increased alertness, strength, endurance—exhilaration
- Gamesmanship and sportsmanship
- Sense of eliteness and desire for recognition
- Sense of purpose
- Increased religious faith
- Personal bonding
- Horizontal and vertical bonding
- Unit identity
- Unit cohesion
- Heroism[2]

Trained Army leaders expect these behaviors from all soldiers. Now look at how you can use each of the positive behaviors that result from stress to achieve excellence.

Increased Alertness, Strength, Endurance— Exhilaration

The human body reacts strongly to the dangers of combat and causes an exhilaration that soldiers describe as a thrill or an adrenaline rush. Soldiers often experience a sense of heightened strength and endurance, and they feel extremely competent. Every war has countless stories of soldiers doing feats far beyond their abilities and performing in spite of otherwise disabling wounds.

Corporations that strive for success can get a sense of this exhilaration in their teams that accomplish very difficult tasks or meet strenuous circumstances head-on. Manufacturing teams that turn out special orders or overcome seemingly impossible equipment failures leave the factory with a feeling of exhilaration. Sales teams that conquer improbable obstacles are ready to take on all competitors. The greater the challenge, the greater the exhilaration experienced.

Gamesmanship and Sportsmanship

Veterans are sometime offended when others refer to combat as a game, but many aspects of battle take on the dynamics of gamesmanship as soldiers hunt down and destroy enemy equipment and personnel. They themselves are pursued as they hunt the enemy, and the consequences of poor performance are deadly; the competitiveness takes on a lethal dimension. Single incidents are threatening enough, but the cumulative stress is magnified for soldiers whose lives are under constant threat—waking, sleeping, eating, and working.

This attitude is also common in corporate battles. As with frontline soldiers and combat service support units, employees who are in direct contact with customers and competitors feel the gamesmanship more than those in support roles. As they play the game, upper management tracks progress on computer printouts much the same way as coaches track the statistics of their team's performance.

Business leaders can use this sense of athletic competition to motivate and encourage excellence as they strive to overwhelm competitors. Try using athletic terminology and record keeping to develop enthusiasm and increase performance among your employees who like the idea of playing a serious game against a dedicated foe.

Sense of Eliteness and Desire for Recognition

The *Leaders' Manual for Combat Stress Control* explains that "Combat veterans who have achieved a high level of combat-stimulated proficiency and self-confidence are likely to consider themselves and their unit elite. They walk with pride and may expect special consideration or deference from others less elite." This stress reaction is useful in battle, but such an attitude can irritate rear-area troops and other units. Commanders who want to avoid serious relationship issues need to be aware of such reactions and ensure fair and uniform treatment of others who consider such an attitude as arrogance. Likewise, if manufacturing, sales, and product management personnel experience a string of successes, they can sometimes appear to be arrogant when interacting with support departments. Managers can control this situation by having open discussions with those involved and reminding them that their successes are impossible without the support of others.

Those who display this positive stress reaction can minimize its negative effect by scheduling time to *visit* with support personnel rather than briefly depositing their requirements before rushing off for another success. Tokens of friendship and recognition also go a long way in avoiding low-level conflicts that can affect success as the organization strives for excellence. Salespeople who use handwritten thank-you notes, personalized e-mail messages, and public commendation of support staff build relationships that pay off in future support requirements.

Official recognition for achievements contributes to the sense of eliteness and encourages others to strive for similar results. Medals are often awarded for service and heroism. Written and verbal commendations and compliments are tools of the trade in the Army and can work just as well in business. Tangible items of recognition are good substitutes for the medals, and certificates and letters of commendation for individuals and teams are extremely valuable to employees and their companies.

Sense of Purpose

A frequent result of the high stress of war with all of its hazards is a sense of patriotism and common purpose that helps everyone overcome the inconsequential discomforts and inconveniences of wartime. The same kind of stress reaction can be seen in the sense of purpose and pride in community recovery efforts after a national disaster.

Corporations see examples of this positive stress reaction when management successfully works through a strike or start-up teams open new operations on schedule. Some companies have energized employee sense of purpose by supporting charities and worthy causes. One technique for developing a sense of purpose is to remind everyone of the value of their participation through newsletters, bulletin board announcements, e-mail, and verbal commendations. Keep the sense of purpose alive through frequent communications. A keen sense of purpose helps organizations significantly in their quest for excellence.

Increased Religious Faith

The September 11, 2001, terrorist attacks on the Pentagon and the World Trade Center destroyed the buildings, killed approximately 3,000 people, and packed our nation's churches, synagogues, and mosques with people searching for spiritual stability. In the following months major media coverage displayed similar reactions among American troops preparing for battle in Afghanistan and Iraq. The hazards of war and other disasters remind people of their spiritual needs. Dedicated believers are encouraged in their faith, and seekers want to find hope in the midst of disaster.

The Army recognizes that the chaos of war challenges religious and spiritual values that form the basis of many soldiers' inner strength and courage. The *Leaders' Manual for Combat Stress Control* describes how ministry teams counsel mild combat fatigue casualties and "prepare soldiers to manage combat stress with training before and during deployment. This training helps the soldier to draw upon spiritual strength and share strength and confidence during intensive combat."

Corporations can help employees by including ministry contingencies in disaster awareness plans, making ministry staff available at all times, and encouraging an atmosphere of acceptance for various faiths. Some companies have even arranged for chaplains to visit their business sites routinely and to make special visits to help employees who want assistance during the hard times of life. The disaster of war or national trauma affects great numbers of people, but individuals have their own tragedies in good times and bad. Recognizing the importance of individual faith provides a sense of stability that can be useful in a company's striving for excellence.

Personal Bonding

The U.S. Army is well known for the strong bonds that form among those soldiers who share the common hazards of combat and realistic training. Living together day after day and the lack of privacy provide an environment for rapid bonding that eliminates stereotypes, prejudices, and personality conflicts. The bonding serves well in times of danger when soldiers sacrifice their own comfort and safety for the welfare of the group. The *Leaders' Manual for Combat Stress Control* concludes "While patriotism and sense of purpose will get American soldiers to the battlefield, the soldiers' own accounts (and many systematic studies) testify that what keeps them there amid the fear of death and mutilation is, above all else, their loyalty to their fellow soldiers."

Similar bonding develops vertically between combat leaders and soldiers who depend on each other for success. Realistic, tough training is also used to create a horizontal bonding between officers and sergeants who lead small units and depend on each other in battle.

Military leaders consider this bonding so important that the entire Army was reorganized in 1986 to bring stability to individual units. Instead of reassigning individuals worldwide, an effort is now made for soldiers to serve with their parent unit for the duration of their enlistment. According to Army regulation AR 600-83, units are held together to "foster a greater sense of belonging and esprit by providing career-long affiliation with a specific Regiment or institution."[2]

Companies with rapid personnel turnover rates lose the bonding so highly valued by the U.S. Army. Low turnover rates, on the other hand, foster the bonding, loyalty, and dedication that can help companies that strive for excellence. You can enhance this bonding in your own company by using the stress-control techniques discussed in this book along with your own team building and positive leadership. Leaders and employees who survive difficult challenges together quickly develop a bond that has the same effect as that found in military units.

Unit Identity and Cohesion

The Army's revised personnel assignment policies also help individuals identify with their units and develop the cohesion that is important in battle. As discussed in earlier chapters, these attributes build esprit de corps and minimize the likelihood of combat fatigue casualties. Soldiers who are dedicated to others in their unit and have pride in their organization are less likely to suffer from the negative stress reactions associated with combat.

Corporations see the same results with long-term employees who are part of the culture. These people tell the stories and uphold the traditions meaningful in their careers. Their participation in all company activities builds identity and cohesion for newer members and enhances their contribution to the company's efforts to succeed.

Heroism

Heroism based on sense of purpose and loyalty to fellow soldiers is the premier positive stress behavior. According to the *Leaders' Manual for Combat Stress Control*, "The ultimate positive combat stress behaviors are acts of heroism." During times of crisis soldiers perform extraordinary acts of strength and bravery, frequently beyond the realm of human understanding. The Army's system of awarding medals and commendations for acts of courage provides well-deserved recognition and encourages similar actions from others. Posthumous awards recognize the sacrifice of heroes who die in their efforts to help others succeed.

Many corporations have unrecognized heroes in their midst. Some of the heroes are humble military veterans who do not reveal their acts of combat courage, and others are heroes who have accomplished great things for the company where they work. In your own company you have people who have performed extraordinarily in developing products, getting sales, cutting costs, improving efficiencies, and so on. Your company is stronger in many ways because of your heroes. Recognizing the efforts of these heroes through company award luncheons, news releases, in-house newsletters, bonuses, and so on will contribute to organizational excellence and encourage others to perform as well.

Leaders Are Also Vulnerable to Stress

Dedicated, loyal, and hardworking corporate leaders are among the heroes discussed here. In a sense, these heroes sacrifice their lives for the benefit of their company and their team of fellow employees, enduring extreme stress for years on end. Many of them spend more hours with the company than with their families. Their personal relationships suffer because of their loyalty to their company or organization.

Possibly, the most difficult stress-control programs are those that leaders must implement for themselves. While these leaders are admired examples of the American work ethic and value system, they have a hard time recognizing their own demise. Positive stress reactions keep them going while negative stress reactions deplete their physical and emotional well-being. Their systems feed on the positive emotions of high stress and obscure the resulting damage to their health.

The following strategies are frequently used by leaders who want to achieve balance and excel in their personal and family lives while guiding their companies to success. As a dedicated leader striving for excellence, look for ways to implement these strategies in your work life.

Teamwork and Delegation

Leaders sometimes take on additional responsibilities without unloading anything. The physical and mental stress becomes a "normal" part of life for these dedicated corporate and military leaders. Stress prevents these leaders from recognizing their own need for assistance and from using team resources and delegating responsibility.

If leaders in this situation permitted others to help them, they would probably find that everyone is ready and willing to contribute to their success. Both teamwork and delegation of responsibilities will help relieve stress and result in better performance. Leaders who go home exhausted at the end of every extended workday need to get an objective evaluation of their stress level and performance. Coworkers see the coming failures of stressed leaders long before the leaders admit to themselves that their work is not quite up to par. Conversations with family members, peers, supervisors, and spiritual consultants can help these leaders get an accurate assessment of just how well they are doing.

Even if you are not among the overstressed who are on the verge of a breakdown, consider implementing the teamwork and delegation approach to alleviate some of the stress you do experience and give yourself some room to maneuver in your ongoing efforts.

Organization, Scheduling, and Time Management

Many leaders found their way up the ladder of success with organizational skills that were adequate in the beginning. Somewhere along the line, however, their promotions exceeded their organizational ability, and they operate on the verge of being out of control. They know about scheduling and time management techniques, but they ignore the more sophisticated tools because they have gotten by, so far, with a simple day-planner.

If you feel the pressure of having too little time or being out of control, you might evaluate the high-tech tools available to help you regain control of these things. These suggestions seem rather elementary to those who have embraced systems such as handheld digital organizers, contact management systems, and e-communications. If you are not using these tools, however, you have been left behind. You must catch up.

Those who once cleverly bragged about being computer illiterate have learned that this remark is no longer acceptable. The same thing is true with other technology. Have you noticed that listeners politely change the subject when you reveal your lack of techno-savvy? Admitting this shortcoming does not help you excel in the business arena.

With only a few formal or informal classes, you can start using some of these tools to reduce your stress level and reestablish your credibility as a competent twenty-first-century leader. Your hectic schedule or lack of confidence is no excuse for not catching up on the high-tech performance curve. If you have succeeded to this point in your life, you have the ability to learn how to use the modern tools of the trade.

Physical Exercise and Health

If you suffer from back pain, frequent or chronic headaches, colon problems, or misplaced irritability and anger, you need a break. These are classic symptoms of stress. Discussing these symptoms with your physician or chiropractor will elicit questions about how things are going at work. Since you don't recognize the symptoms of stress in yourself or because of your pride of accomplishment, you will likely respond that things are busy but not actually stressful.

Try looking in the mirror and convincing yourself of that response. You are probably overly stressed and just do not know what to do about it. You have worked so hard for so long to get where you are that you do not want to take a chance on disturbing your success. In the meantime, you are killing yourself. This form of suicide takes a lot longer than some of the more graphic methods, but it is just as deadly. Soon you will find that your immune system has deteriorated; you have compromised your heart, circulatory, and nervous systems; and medication and surgery are just around the corner.

If you recognize that stress is a factor in your life, you can take action to limit its effects. An exercise routine that gives you at least a thirty-minute aerobic workout, three to four times a week is a great way to start limiting what stress does to your body. Medical literature tells us that walking is just as effective as vigorous exercise programs. But leaders who get into this stress predicament are usually the ones who enjoy aggressive exercise, such as bicycling, swimming, or running. They just feel that the high-energy programs accomplish more.

I recognize myself in the stress-filled situations discussed here. The Army welcomed my overachieving personality and gave me assignments to match my desire to succeed. After U.S. Army Ranger school and a command assignment in Europe, I was assigned to combat duty as an infantry company commander in Vietnam.

If I'd known then what I know now, the outcome would have been different the night I led a six-man reconnaissance patrol into the middle of a coastal village. Our encounter with a group of about forty Vietcong soldiers started with a standing-in-the-open-looking-at-each-other gunfight reminiscent of some of Hollywood's famous cowboy gunfights. As a flare lit up the night sky, the enemy and I stood facing each other no more than ten feet apart. He was as surprised as I was and swung his rifle toward me. As my mind raced to find a way to defuse the situation, our bodies reacted automatically just as we had been trained. With the first rounds fired, I was wounded and knocked unconscious. When I awoke and tried to crawl to safety, I was wounded again—the first time in my left leg and the second just above my right ear.

After several weeks, my condition was stable enough to permit amputation of my leg below the knee, and I began what was to be a yearlong period of recovery. At the end of that time, I convinced the colonel in charge of infantry assignments to allow me to continue on active duty. The colonel, Norman Schwartzkopf, later gained fame as the Allied commander in Desert Storm, our first war with Iraq, but he was my hero from the moment he uncharacteristically approved my waiver to continue on active duty.

After several more years in the Army, a number of university teaching positions, a stint with two Fortune 500 companies, and a period of time leading an international charity, I discovered that I'd spent thirty-five years at sedentary office work and modest activities. To turn things around, I undertook a treadmill regimen and worked my way up to running three miles a day.

The renewed running program became an essential in my daily activities. I was not satisfied with three times a week and tried to get to the gym every day. To my amazement, my chronic back pain disappeared where years of chiropractic adjustments had failed. Other stress symptoms disappeared, and my health and sense of well-being improved dramatically.

If you have some of the typical stress symptoms, you do not need further details about how exercise will assist you. You just need to break your routine, decide you will put up with the good-natured jests about your change of lifestyle, and try something. Just pick a routine and go to it. You can change it later if you want to try something else, but in the meantime, you will build a new set of habits and your stress levels will drop significantly. Regardless of your age or ailments, this is going to help you, and you'll enjoy it if you give it a chance.

Outside Interests

Maintaining an interest in subjects outside your work arena is another healthy way to reduce stress and renew some unused brain synapses. If you spend your days at a desk or in meetings with the same kinds of people about the same old subject, you will easily benefit from new activities. Just as exercise helps reduce the physical effects of stress, involvement in new activities engages your mind and reduces many other negative stress reactions.

One good place to start is with those hobbies you left behind because of your heavy workload. Dust off the hobby and schedule some time for it. If you no longer have the passion for these hobbies, try something else.

If your interests lie in helping others, there are plenty of opportunities to volunteer at your church or community charities. Getting involved with the extreme needs of average Americans will do wonders for stress. When you find out how little money and resources people have at the bottom of the social structure, you will go back to work with greater appreciation of the routine that has grown old.

If your outside interest is an independent business, you will find a second source of stress relief in the security it brings. Even if the business income is small in comparison to your regular job, you will have something to fall back on if a corporate restructuring displaces you.

Because you have a strong affinity for your work, you can provide some relief by expanding your base of knowledge with more research and education. While it will not have the same effect as a true outside interest, new approaches to industry involvement will renew your enthusiasm, broaden your perspective, and give you new things to think about.

Spiritual

You have seen how spiritual stability is important to soldiers and corporate employees; this aspect is not just for subordinates. An understanding of a higher power brings a lot of stress relief. Some religions and denominations are more academic and others are more personal, but whatever your beliefs, you owe it to yourself to renew your involvement at this stage of your life.

If you have read every other chapter in this book, you are searching for ways to interrupt this seemingly unending cycle of stress. You are overworked. Your stress level is affecting your health. You are tired of the same old job. In fact, you have thought about changing jobs but felt the stress would just be too much.

You should realize that your success is limited in some ways and that you cannot overcome some of those insurmountable obstacles. You cannot continue with things the way they are. Things are not going to change if you do not take action.

The most difficult part of reengaging in your spiritual beliefs is the change of character you will display to family members and others close to you. The expectations of others are a powerful force, but they will admire your decisions even if they do temporarily make clever remarks about your changes. This concerns your stress, your health, and your efforts to regain control in your life. If you think a change in spiritual activity is needed, give it a try.

Family

The Army has a fully developed program for assisting families of soldiers stationed in the United States and overseas. Military leaders know that family concerns drive stress levels way up, so formal programs go to great lengths to provide information and training for everyone concerned.

Your family is no different. Things just do not work the same way when you are away on business—either for travel or long hours at the office. Your family needs you, and you need your family. You might be accustomed to such a level of stress that you cannot recognize this, but it is true. Neither your wealth nor your material items will replace the leadership and companionship that you bring to your family when you are present.

Your job requires more than the standard forty hours a week, but you are very successful in figuring out how to do things. You are creative. You know how to work the system. You are smart enough to direct some of this high IQ to the benefit of your family. For your own sake and your family, you are capable of ending your day at 4:30 p.m. instead of 6:00 p.m.—just put it on your calendar and make it a priority.

All of those urgent things you do in the late afternoon will be there waiting for you when you come in the next day. If they were truly urgent, you would have taken care of them much earlier. Put some of those papers in a stack for doing later and sift through them a month later. You will throw away 80 or 90 percent of what you once thought was important.

As you are reintroduced to your family members, you will be surprised at how capable they are. You will learn about their ambitions, and their problems. You probably have some of the answers they need for life.

Success Under Fire

The battles and heroes described in *Winning Under Fire* are only here to illustrate the points of each chapter. All of them are part of history. In the world where you operate, you are one of the heroes, and people are counting on you.

You are just as much a leader as any of the military heroes. You can influence activities and outcomes. You have the ability to influence lives. You can motivate people to success. You can reduce the stressors that are internal to your company. You can help people reduce the stressors that they bring from home.

You can use these Army strategies to encourage greater success and to minimize the negative stress reactions that many employees are experiencing. Regardless of your own concern for employees as individuals, your company needs their expertise and full participation. You can influence this by pursuing stress control as you would any other opportunity.

Furthermore, you can act to control the stress in your own life and maximize your own value to your company. If your own stress is under control, you will be more effective in doing your job and in reducing the effects of stress throughout the organization. It really does not matter which Army strategy you employ first, just take the one that seems the most appropriate and begin your journey of winning under fire.

Notes

1. Army field manual FM 22-51, *Leaders' Manual for Combat Stress Control*, Headquarters, Department of the Army, Washington, D.C., September 29, 1994. The positive stress behaviors and the descriptions are also summarized from FM 22-51.
2. Army regulation AR 600-83, "The New Manning System—COHORT Unit Replacement System," Department of the Army, Washington, D.C., 27 October 1986.

INDEX

ABOUT THE AUTHOR

In addition to owning and operating his own business, Dale Collie's corporate experience includes several years in sales and distribution management with Fortune 500 textile and chemical companies, servicing customers throughout the United States, Canada, and Mexico. His international work also includes starting businesses in Ukraine as well as export sales to South America, Asia, and the Caribbean.

His efforts to implement Total Quality Management helped these companies succeed in the face of stiff competition, gaining market share and increasing profits in spite of down markets, foreign imports, and geographic obstacles.

This corporate experience provided the background for Dale's leadership role in guiding a near-bankrupt charity into a $37 million operation in just seven years. *Fast Company* magazine recognized him as one of America's Fast 50 innovative leaders for the turn-around effort and rapid growth of service to the homeless, the hungry, and the impoverished in the United States and Eastern Europe.

Prior to his work in the corporate and nonprofit communities, Dale's military experience included service as a U.S. Army Ranger and command of troops in Europe and Vietnam. He survived combat wounds and gained approval to stay on active duty as an amputee, proving the importance of perseverance and self-confidence. Other interesting assignments included a tour of duty with the Armor School think tank at Fort Knox, Kentucky, service as an aide-de-camp for a general officer, and responsibilities as an Inspector General.

Dale has also taught business communications, public speaking, and English at the University of Kentucky, Indiana Wesleyan University, and the United States Military Academy at West Point, New York.

Through these various adventures, he has learned that the long-term stress in corporate assignments is just as great a health and productivity factor as stress experienced in military training and combat. Of course, the dangers of combat exceed the hazards of corporate work, but the continuous, day-to-day reaction to corporate stress can take its toll in both arenas.

Additional stories about how Dale has used his military experience in the corporate setting can be found in his book *Frontline Leadership: From War Room to Boardroom—Corporate Leadership Lessons Learned in Combat*. Stories about how he used his corporate and military experience in guiding a nonprofit corporation and helping people in need can be found in *Conversations on Faith* that he coauthored with Robert Schuller, Tony Campolo, and Jennifer O'Neill.

In addition to being a consultant, coach, and advisor to business leaders, Dale is a professional speaker, helping leaders and managers get the best from their key people. His keynotes, seminars, and retreats focus on leadership, communications, and stress control. You can contact him at collie@couragebuilders.com or by phone at 877-826-5543. His website is www.couragebuilders.com.